QUEERS THE WORD

Queer Theology
.com

Copyright 2020 © Brian G. Murphy and Shannon TL Kearns; BMSK Creative LLC

Copyright allows us to do this work. Thank you for buying an authorized copy of this book and for supporting our work by complying with copyright laws by not reproducing, scanning, or distributing any part of this book without prior permission.

Unless otherwise noted, Bible quotations are from the Common English Bible and used by permission. Copyright 2012 by Common English Bible and/or its suppliers. All rights reserved.

NIV quotations are from THE HOLY BIBLE, NEW INTERNATIONAL VERSION®, NIV® Copyright © 1973, 1978, 1984, 2011 by Biblica, Inc.® Used by permission. All rights reserved worldwide.

NRSV quotations are from New Revised Standard Version Bible, copyright © 1989 National Council of the Churches of Christ in the United States of America. Used by permission. All rights reserved worldwide.

ESV quotations are from ESV® Bible (The Holy Bible, English Standard Version®), copyright © 2001 by Crossway, a publishing ministry of Good News Publishers. Used by permission. All rights reserved

To every LGBTQ+ person over the years, decades, centuries, millennia who has lived, died, fought, hoped, prayed, grieved, and thrived: We all reflect the image of God. May you always remember that.

CONTENTS

	Introduction	1
1.	**Returning Another Way** » Matthew 2:1-12	5
2.	**You Are Very Good** » Genesis 1-2	8
3.	**Test Everything**† » 1 Thessalonians 5:21	10
4.	**Pay Attention To Me*** » Psalm 55	12
5.	**Mary, The Badass Mother of God** » Mark 6:1-13, Luke 10:1-24	14
6.	**Good Fruit** » Matthew 7:1-20	16
7.	**The Lord's Prayer** » Matthew 6:5-14	18
8.	**A Name Greater Than Son or Daughter** » Isaiah 56:1-8	20
9.	**What Does Palm Sunday Look Like Today?** » Matthew 21:1-7	22
10.	**A Depressed Prophet** » 1 Kings 19	25
11.	**Jesus Still Had His Scars*** » John 20:19-29	28
12.	**Fight For Your Faith** » Genesis 32	30
13.	**The Body of Christ Has AIDS** » 1 Corinthians 12:1-31	32
14.	**Christ's Temptation, Our Liberation** » Luke 4	35
15.	**Family*** » Mark 3:20-35	38
16.	**Why Did Jesus Come?** » John 10:7-21	40
17.	**Down But Not Destroyed** » 2 Corinthians 4:8-13	43
18.	**Doers Of The Word** » James 1:19-27	46
19.	**Your Body Is A Temple**† » 1 Corinthians 6:12-20	48
20.	**Reaping The Harvest** » Psalm 126	50

21.	**I Am A Sodomite** †
» Genesis 19:1-28 & Ezekiel 16:49-50	52
22.	**Come and See** » John 1:31-51	54
23.	**Word Became Flesh** †
» John 1:14, John 14:16-17, Acts 2:1-4	56
24.	**Offer Your Body** † » Romans 12	59
25.	**What Are You Building On?*** » Luke 6:39-49	62
26.	**Fire In My Bones** » Jeremiah 20:7-18	64
27.	**The One That Was Tossed Away*** » 1 Peter 2	66
28.	**Honoring Marriage & Family** » Hebrews 13:1-16	68
29.	**Community** » Hebrews 10:22-25	71
30.	**God's Good News** » Isaiah 61	74
31.	**Rest** » Matthew 11:1-10, 28-30	76
32.	**The Wicked & The Righteous** » Matthew 25:31-46	79
33.	**Jesus Comes Out** » Matthew 17:1-13	82
34.	**Shake Them Off & Leave Them Behind**
» Matthew 10:5-15, Mark 6:1-13, Luke 10:1-24	84
35.	**With His Body** » Ephesians 2:11-22	86
36.	**What God Has Made Clean** » Acts 10	88
37.	**Come Alive, Dry Bones** » Ezekiel 37:1-14	90
38.	**What Is Worship?** » Amos 5	92
39.	**Spiritual Hunger** » Acts 8:26-40	94
40.	**Nothing Can Separate You From God's Love**
» Romans 8:18-39	96
	Next steps on your journey	99
	More About The Authors & QueerTheology.com	100

Entries marked with a * *symbol were written by Fr. Shannon TL Kearns, entries marked with a* † *symbol were written by Brian G. Murphy*

Introduction

Over the years, one of the more frequent requests we've gotten at QueerTheology.com is for recommendations for a good, queer affirming, daily devotional. People wanted something that allowed them to spend time with Scripture every day. We looked for devotionals to recommend, but almost all of the ones we found were either anti-gay in their theology, specifically for heterosexual couples, or based on something other than the Bible.

We tried to meet the need with our Daily Affirmations project, but over and over we've heard, "We want more." We want more Bible. We want something we can hold in our hands. We want something where we don't need to translate the theology or switch the pronouns.

There was nothing for us to recommend, so we decided to create the resource we were all longing for.

What you hold in your hands is a 40-day devotional. It's designed with one entry per day. They aren't dated, so you can start whenever you pick it up, and if you miss a day (or more), you won't get behind.

Each entry is based on a Bible passage. There are options for reading the whole passage, or just a portion, in case you're short on time. Then there is a short reflection written either by Fr. Shay or Brian that puts the passage in the context of queer theology and lives. Finally, there are some prompts for journaling and some action items so you can put your faith to work in the world. Don't feel the need to respond to every prompt and do every action for every day. Pick the ones that excite you the most (and maybe some that scare you too).

We hope this devotional meets a great need for our community, enriches your faith life, and helps you grow (or encounter) your love for Scripture.

Peace on your journey,
Fr. Shay and Brian
Co-founders of QueerTheology.com

The Devotions

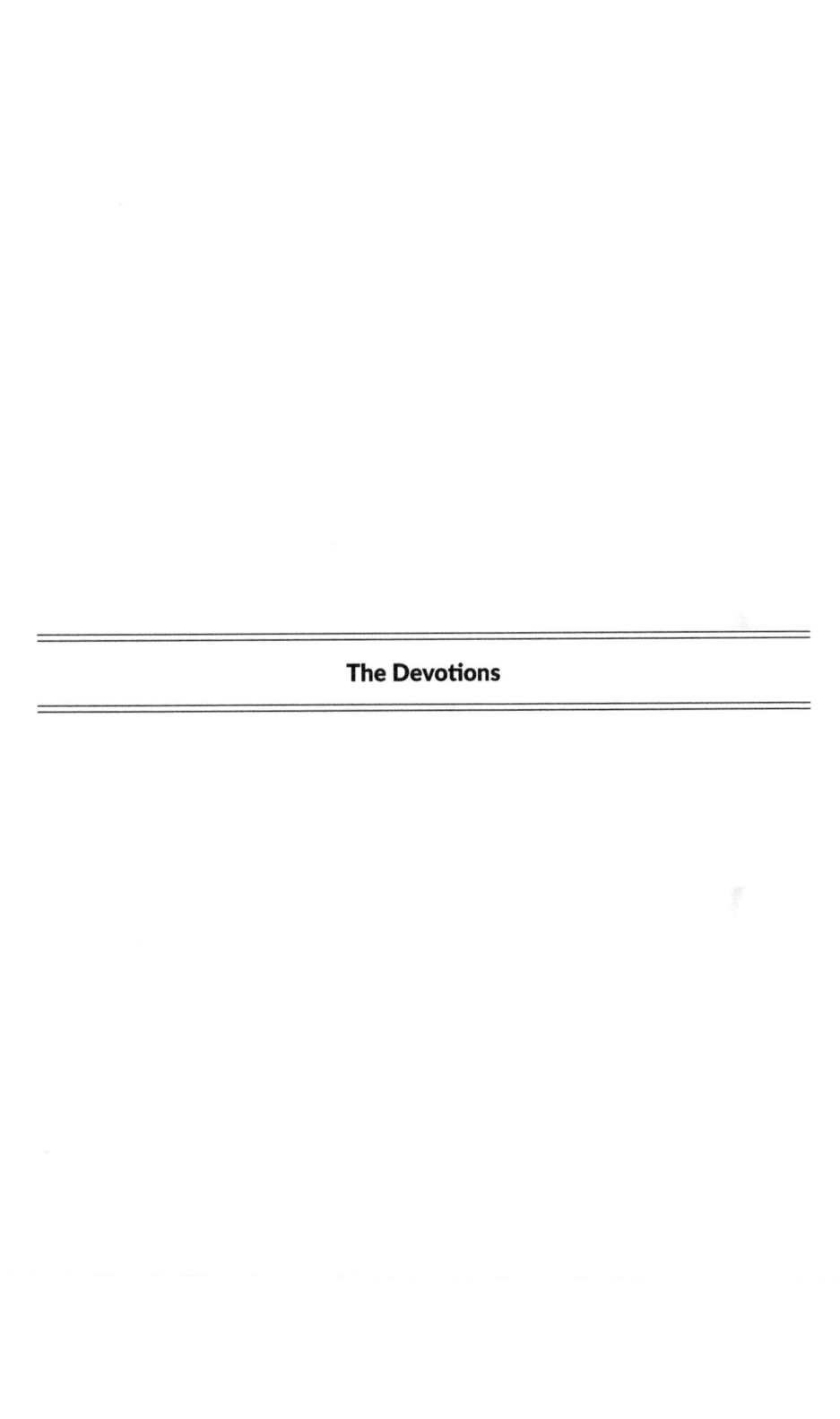

Day One
Returning Another Way

If you have time, read MATTHEW 2:1-12 in your favorite Bible translation then come back to this page.

If you're short on time, read this and pay attention to what jumps out at you as you read:

> *On coming to the house, they saw the child with his mother Mary, and they bowed down and worshiped him. Then they opened their treasures and presented him with gifts of gold, frankincense and myrrh. And having been warned in a dream not to go back to Herod, they returned to their country by another route.*
> **Matthew 2:11-12**

THE SCENE OF THE "WISE MEN" COMING TO VISIT THE BABY JESUS is imprinted on our collective consciousness—whether from church pagents or Christmas movies or front yard nativity scenes. In most tellings of this tale, the wise men are supporting characters. They are there to reinforce the magnificence of Jesus. They arrive and then they disappear, never to be heard from again. The story of Matthew's Gospel follows Jesus, not these travelers.

But let's stick with them for a moment.

These Magi (whom patriarchy reinterprets as men) see a new star in the sky and are moved to find out what it means.

They set out to find the one whose birth the star announces. And they find Jesus.

The author of Matthew's Gospel is laying out his case that right from the beginning, there was something special about Jesus. Even Magi in a foreign land recognized him as King of the Jews. Jesus, not Caesar, is king, the gospel writer is emphasizing here; a treasonous claim.

The wise travelers could have encountered the baby Jesus and gone back home, from whence they came. That's what many of us do. For instance, we are stirred to attend a Black Lives Matter march or Pride protest by current events, and then a few months later, our lives slide back to normal.

That's not what happens here, though. The Magi have an encounter with Jesus that so transforms them that they cannot possibly go home the way they came. They are changed. They "returned by another route."

Has that happened to you? You encountered something so meaningful that you could not help but be changed by it? Your life could not help but be eternally altered?

Perhaps it was the first time you met a trans person and you realized "Hot damn! That could be me?!"

Or maybe it was an injustice that cemented your calling as an activist or ally.

Perhaps it was your first queer kiss, when you realized there was no denying it any longer.

We are all shaped by our life experiences. With a little bit of distance, we can sometimes see just how big a difference the smallest moment made. In the hustle and bustle of life, it's easy to miss them, to let them pass by without a second thought.

What if you took some time to see—truly see—the moments that shaped you? To think about that time on the dance floor or the church retreat or the picket line or summer camp or whatever it might be for you. And to name it holy. To remember that there you encountered the divine and were forever changed.

These moments aren't limited to your past. There are "manger moments" waiting ahead of you, if only you'll pay attention. If only you'll see the star in the sky and follow your curiosity and see where it leads and be open to being transformed by what you find there.

Onward you go, in a new direction.

Journal Prompts

- What is a moment in your life that changed the course you were on?
- Has there been a time when you were so changed by something you "returned another way?"
- What do you think happened to the Magi after they got home?

Actions

- Go on a walk — or take a trip however you are able to get around — to somewhere familiar; then, on your walk home, go a way you haven't been before. Notice what comes up for you as you return another way.
- Make a mental list of all the people, places, and experiences that have shaped who you are. After each one, say to yourself "God was there and so was I."

Day Two
You Are Very Good

If you have time, read GENESIS 1-2 in your favorite Bible translation then come back to this page.

If you're short on time, read this and pay attention to what jumps out at you as you read:

> *Then God said, "Let us make humanity in our image to resemble us so that they may take charge of the fish of the sea, the birds in the sky, the livestock, all the earth, and all the crawling things on earth."*
>
> *God created humanity in God's own image,*
> *in the divine image God created them,*
> *male and female God created them.*
>
> *God blessed them and said to them, "Be fertile and multiply; fill the earth and master it. Take charge of the fish of the sea, the birds in the sky, and everything crawling on the ground." Then God said, "I now give to you all the plants on the earth that yield seeds and all the trees whose fruit produces its seeds within it. These will be your food. To all wildlife, to all the birds in the sky, and to everything crawling on the ground—to everything that breathes—I give all the green grasses for food." And that's what happened. God saw everything he had made: it was supremely good.*
>
> **Genesis 1: 26-31**

FOR MANY OF US WHO ARE QUEER, we read this passage in Genesis with trepidation because "God made Adam and Eve, not Adam and Steve." Or if we're trans, we read this as God creating binary absolute genders that leave no space for us. But what if we could read this passage differently?

In this passage we have a God who looks at everything God has made so far and still isn't satisfied. God wants to create another creature, this time one that reflects the very image of the Divine. And so God creates two beings in order to reflect the multi-facetedness of God's identity. And God looks and declares these humans "very good." Not just okay, not just good, but very good.

The writers of Genesis weren't trying to write a science textbook or explain marriage. They were getting at something much deeper, the truth of identity: You were created to be in community with other people and with the Divine.

These identities we have aren't barriers to those relationships, they are, instead, reflections of the many faces of the Divine. When we each bring our whole selves to the community, we are creating something that is closer to showing the world the true face of God.

Journal Prompts

- ❖ What does this reframing do to your understanding of this passage?
- ❖ How does it feel to think of yourself as **very good**?
- ❖ How does thinking about community as a reflection of God resonate with you?

Action Items

- ❖ Post a selfie on social media with the caption "I am made in the image of God and I am VERY GOOD."
- ❖ Look at yourself in the mirror and say "I bear the image of the Divine."
- ❖ Draw or collage a self portrait that portrays your many identities. Somewhere on it write "I was created in the Divine Image."

Day Three
Test Everything

If you have time, read 1 THESSALONIANS 5:12-28 in your favorite Bible translation then come back to this page.

If you're short on time, read this and pay attention to what jumps out at you as you read:

Test everything; hold fast to that which is good.

1 Thessalonians 5:21

QUESTIONING AUTHORITY can sometimes feel like a betrayal. Whether it's our parent, our teacher, our country, or our pastor, we've been told to honor and respect those "above" us, and often "honor and respect" gets translated into "obey without question." That works well in churches and communities where unity is valued above all else. But is life really uniform? Doesn't our lived experience—and the record of the Bible—testify to remarkable diversity?

Imagine a world where no one questioned "what everyone knows" about the Earth's position in the universe, about humanity's ability to fly, or about how disease is spread?

Imagine a world where "Caesar is Lord" was never questioned.

Doubt and questioning, complexity and uncertainty are central to the human experience, whether we are talking about science or faith. This passage reminds us that to question is to be faithful. For a faith to be strong, there must be room for questions and doubt.

LGBTQ+ Christians have too often been told that our lives, loves, and bodies are sick and sinful. Or, perhaps, judgment is dressed up with a friendly smile: "It's a result of the fall," or, "It's ok if you can't help it, but it's just not God's best." Questioning what we've been taught about ourselves is one way we honor God and honor our faith.

Journal Prompts

- How is or was conformity rewarded in the family or communities you have been part of?
- What are some times that going against the grain has led to important breakthroughs?
- What comes up for you if you think about "questioning" as an expression of faithfulness?
- What are some long-held beliefs of yours? What questions might you ask of them?

Action Items

- Search out a community of people who are asking hard questions about faith.
- Share with a friend something you've been thinking through and ask them what they think.
- Make a list of favorite activities, foods, media, and rituals. As you push yourself to question your beliefs, return to some of these comforting practices.

Day Four
Pay Attention To Me

If you have time, read PSALM 55 in your favorite Bible translation then come back to this page.

If you're short on time, read this and pay attention to what jumps out at you as you read:

> *God, listen to my prayer;*
> *don't avoid my request!*
> *Pay attention! Answer me!*
> *I can't sit still while complaining.*
> *I'm beside myself*
> *over the enemy's noise,*
> *at the wicked person's racket,*
> *because they bring disaster on me*
> *and harass me furiously.*

Pslam 55:1-3

WHAT I LOVE ABOUT THE PSALMS is that they don't back down from the full range of human emotion. Psalm 55 is an angsty, demanding, rage-filled request for God to pay attention and bring down enemies. For those of us who grew up in traditions where we were taught to be nice and polite, or to always put on a happy face, reading this Psalm can feel uncomfortable and disorienting.

And yet, Psalms like this teach us there is space in a faithful life for anger, for rage, for demanding. There is space to be fully human and lament. There is space for the marginalized to be angry at the people who oppress them.

What might be different in your life if you made space for your grief? For your anger? For rage? For lament? How might sitting with hard emotions open you up and make you more whole and healthy?

Where might your honesty lead you?

Journal Prompts

- What is something you want God to listen to today?
- Journal about a time when you felt God's silence. What did it feel like?
- What role does lament play in your faith?

Action Items

- Make room for lament in your faith life. This could look like a list in your journal, a jar filled with notes about things that make you upset, an anger corner in your yard where you break old plates.
- Write your own Psalm listing your grievances.

Day Five
Mary, The Badass Mother of God

If you have time, read LUKE 1:46-55 in your favorite Bible translation then come back to this page.

If you're short on time, read this and pay attention to what jumps out at you as you read:

> *He has shown strength with his arm. He has scattered those with arrogant thoughts and proud inclinations. He has pulled the powerful down from their thrones and lifted up the lowly. He has filled the hungry with good things and sent the rich away empty-handed.*
>
> **Luke 1:51-53**

DIFFERENT CHRISTIAN TRADITIONS TEACH DIFFERENT THINGS ABOUT MARY, the mother of Jesus. In some, she is revered; in others, she is almost an afterthought. As you read this passage—this song Mary sings after she is visited by the angel and consents to giving birth—notice how strong she is. This is a Mary who knows her mind and who knows her God.

Mary sings about a God who cares for the poor, who overturns the oppressors, who rights the world. This is the song she was singing even as Jesus was growing in her womb. Is it any wonder that he grew up and said similar things?

Mary raised her son in the tradition she knew, taught him about the God that she knew, and instilled in him a passion for justice. Jesus's entire identity was formed in the community he came from, led by his mother. So when he started to proclaim and preach the Kingdom of God, those beliefs came from how he was raised.

For some of us, the traditions in which we were raised don't bring the same kind of life and faith that Mary passed on to Jesus. For us, we need to re-learn and re-explore and find new community and new beliefs. For others, we might need to revisit what we loved about the faith we grew up in, to go more deeply into the traditions in which we were raised because we know they can continue to give us life.

Whether you need to re-learn or just dive deeper, spend some time reflecting on the faith of your childhood today and finding a way forward.

Journal Prompts

- Does this reflection shift how you think of Mary?
- How does the faith formation you received as a child influence your life today?
- Are there any places in your faith that you want to learn more about?

Action Items

- Write your own hymn, song, or poem describing what you believe about God.
- Do one thing today to bring about more justice in the world. This could be making a donation, signing a petition, writing a letter, going to a meeting, finding a place to volunteer. The options are endless! Just pick one!
- Pick one of the places in your faith that you want to learn more about that you identified in your journaling and do some digging into what there might be to learn!

Day Six
Good Fruit

If you have time, read MATTHEW 7:1-20 in your favorite Bible translation then come back to this page.

If you're short on time, read this and pay attention to what jumps out at you as you read:

> *"Watch out for false prophets. They come to you in sheep's clothing, but inwardly they are ferocious wolves. By their fruit you will recognize them. Do people pick grapes from thorn bushes, or figs from thistles? Likewise, every good tree bears good fruit, but a bad tree bears bad fruit. A good tree cannot bear bad fruit, and a bad tree cannot bear good fruit. Every tree that does not bear good fruit is cut down and thrown into the fire. Thus, by their fruit you will recognize them.*
>
> **Matthew 7:15-20**

THERE ARE A LOT OF DIFFERENT WAYS TO BE CHRISTIAN. There are Christian leaders proclaiming wildly different messages, from Joel Osteen to Martin Luther King Jr. to Mother Teresa to Dietrich Bonhoeffer to Jerry Falwell to Troy Perry to us.

How are you to know whom to trust?

Jesus anticipated this during his lifetime. He knew he couldn't live forever, and he trusted that his ministry and movement would continue on after him. So how would his earliest followers—and those followers decades, centuries, and even millennia later—know whom and what to trust?

Well, in Matthew 7, Jesus offered us all a paradigm for discernment: "When confronted with a teaching, look at the results of that theology. You'll be able to tell," he is urging us.

When it comes to LGBTQ+ lives and Christianity, you may hear different things:

"Your queerness is a sin! Repent!"

"You might not have chosen it, but you'll need to be celibate and you shouldn't transition."

"If you can twist yourself into a close approximation of traditional, Christian, heterosexual monogamy, it's OK to be gay and have a same-gender spouse."

"Queerness is a good and holy part of the diversity of God's creation."

So, look at the fruits. What do they bear?

The fruits of anti-LGBTQ theology reveal its falseness: depression, despair, suicide, fractured families, loss of faith, bullying, harassment.

The fruits of affirming theology testify to its rightness: a return to faith, a healing of relationships, and a vibrance and resurgence in church life.

We see the good fruits of affirming theology in all aspects of life: from thriving faith communities to psychological well-being to healthy and stable families. It's true on the macro, "researchable" level and it's true on the personal level, too.

Accepting, affirming, celebrating queerness bears good fruit. It's a feast, and you're invited.

Journal Prompts

- ❖ What are beliefs that you hold (or held at one time) that provoke anxiety or despair in you?
- ❖ What are beliefs that you hold that inspire joy?
- ❖ Are there any beliefs you're struggling with? What kind of fruit do they bear in your life?

Action Items

- ❖ Pick an LGBTQ novel, movie, TV show, podcast, or YouTuber to read/watch/listen to. Pay attention to you learn from the stories.
- ❖ Make a list of the "bad fruit" that was present in your life as a result of unaffirming theology. Make a list of the "good fruit" you see in your life and the lives of LGBTQ+ people you know. Burn, shred, or bury the bad fruit. Frame or tack up the list of good fruit.

Day Seven
The Lord's Prayer

If you have time, read MATTHEW 6:5-14 in your favorite Bible translation then come back to this page.

If you're short on time, read this and pay attention to what jumps out at you as you read:

> *Our Father in heaven,*
> *hallowed be your name,*
> *your kingdom come,*
> *your will be done,*
> *   on earth as it is in heaven.*
> *Give us today our daily bread.*
> *And forgive us our debts,*
> *   as we also have forgiven our debtors.*
> *And lead us not into temptation,*
> *   but deliver us from the evil one.*
> *For if you forgive other people when they sin against you, your heavenly Father will also forgive you. But if you do not forgive others their sins, your Father will not forgive your sins.*
>
> **Matthew 6:9-14**

"THE LORD'S PRAYER" is one of the most famous sayings in all of Christianity, possibly in all of the world. You may even know it by heart.

What has become for many a rote recitation, something you can say without even paying attention to the words, is a deeply revolutionary declaration. There is a whole lot packed in here.

First, "your kingdom come, your will be done, on earth as it is in heaven." This sets the stage for everything else that follows (and for the whole of our faith, really): we are not praying in anticipation of some future paradise, we are calling into being a new way of being here and now.

And what is God's will? Here, Matthew tells us, Jesus emphasizes that all should be fed, that debts should be canceled, and that we should forgive each other.

It's clear we are to be active participants here. *We* must forgive debts. *We* must pardon sins. *We* are co-creating "the kingdom of God on earth as it is in heaven."

"Social justice" isn't some add-on to Christianity, it's at the very heart of it. Imprint these words on your heart: on earth as it is in heaven.

On earth.

Here. Now. Today. Let us make it so.

Journal Prompts

- ❖ What changes for you as this prayer shifts from a theological prayer to a call for embodied change?
- ❖ What are some tangible ways you can forgive debts and sins, help people get their daily bread, and otherwise co-create the kingdom of God on earth? Brainstorm them here!

Action Items

- ❖ Forgive someone's debts. This can be any debt owed to you. Let the person know you are releasing the obligation. Or you can help forgive debts owed to others. Help a friend or family member pay off their debts or find an organization that handles debt relief and make a contribution.
- ❖ Contribute to your local food bank.
- ❖ Donate to a transgender person's GoFundMe. Because of employment, housing, and healthcare discrimination, many transgender people need to use GoFundMe in order to get their basic needs met. Ask your friends if they know of anyone in need or search "transgender gofundme" on Twitter, and you'll find many.
- ❖ Find a quiet room where you can be along and recite, out loud or silently, this passage each morning for a week. Pay attention to the thoughts and feelings that come up for you as a result.

Day Eight
A Name Greater Than Son or Daughter

If you have time, read Isaiah 56:1-8 in your favorite Bible translation then come back to this page.

If you're short on time, read this and pay attention to what jumps out at you as you read:

> *The Lord says:*
> *To the eunuchs who keep my sabbaths,*
> *choose what I desire,*
> *and remain loyal to my covenant.*
> *In my temple and courts, I will give them*
> *a monument and a name better than sons and daughters.*
> *I will give to them an enduring name*
> *that won't be removed.*
>
> **Isaiah 56:4-5**

This section of the book of Isaiah is written as the scattered tribes of Israel are being brought back from exile. They are, in many ways, a changed people. Many of their number have been in captivity for years and years. Some of the people have never known freedom. They have no idea of what things were like "before". Others have married and had children far away from their homeland. So where, now, was home?

In the midst of all of this they are able to resume many of their religious practices as free people for the first time. But the temple has been destroyed. And so many of their spiritual practices feel punishing now. Especially these rules mentioned here: about foreigners and eunuchs. Foreigners and eunuchs were forbidden from the religious inner circle. But the realities of exile now mean that there are a whole lot more eunuchs and foreigners than there were before. People who have been made eunuchs while in exile must have felt an even greater sense of loss as they considered that now they were free but excluded from their religious home.

But instead of reiterating the laws, God gives a word of hope. Not only will these people not be cast out and further cut off, they will be given names better than sons and daughters.

For those of us who have changed our names, or come out and been banished from our families or churches of origin, this passage has a word of hope for us, too: in God's community there is an expanded welcome, a place for us, and a name that will be cherished and honored.

Journal Prompts:

- ❖ Think about what your name means to you (whether it was given to you or you chose it yourself). What meaning does it hold? What does your name tell you about yourself and where you came from?
- ❖ What communities have you felt excluded from? What communities have you felt welcomed in?
- ❖ What does it mean to have a name better than "son or daughter"?

Action items:

- ❖ Find a trans person in your life and give them something with their new name on it (or buy something for yourself with your name on it).
- ❖ Create a collage that represents your name and what it means to you.
- ❖ Donate a book about the importance of pronouns to your church or school library.

Day Nine
What does Palm Sunday look like today?

If you have time, read MATTHEW 21:1-17 in your favorite Bible translation then come back to this page.

If you're short on time, read this and pay attention to what jumps out at you as you read:

> *When they approached Jerusalem and came to Bethphage on the Mount of Olives, Jesus gave two disciples a task. He said to them, "Go into the village over there. As soon as you enter, you will find a donkey tied up and a colt with it. Untie them and bring them to me." ...*
>
> *Now a large crowd spread their clothes on the road. Others cut palm branches off the trees and spread them on the road. The crowds in front of him and behind him shouted, "Hosanna to the Son of David! Blessings on the one who comes in the name of the Lord! Hosanna in the highest!"* ...
>
> *Then Jesus went into the temple and threw out all those who were selling and buying there. He pushed over the tables used for currency exchange and the chairs of those who sold doves. He said to them, "It's written, My house will be called a house of prayer. But you've made it a hideout for crooks."*
>
> **Matthew 21:1-2, 8-9, 12-13**

WHAT DOES PALM SUNDAY LOOK LIKE AT YOUR CHURCH? Perhaps it's a parade of children, idyllically waving palm branches. Maybe there is an organ playing a processional. Or conversely, maybe your Palm Sunday experience is one of solemn sermons. Perhaps you don't go to church and have no idea what a Palm Sunday service might be like.

It wasn't like any of that.

In Matthew's telling of it, Jesus's entry into Jerusalem comes toward the end of his ministry. He's been traveling around the Middle East proclaiming his vision of a different kind of Kingdom than the Roman Empire they were living under: a vision of breaking prisoners out of jail, healing the sick, and providing for everyone. A Kingdom where the meek are celebrated, peace is cherished, and the neglected are prioritized.

Now, together with a growing following, Jesus sets his path toward Jerusalem, the epicenter of Jewish life. That religious and political importance meant that Jerusalem was also a city that the Roman occupiers were keen to keep subdued.

As the Passover approaches, Pontius Pilate and a legion of Roman soldiers are dispatched to Jerusalem to "keep the peace" and prevent any uprisings.[1]

Does that sound familiar to you? It calls to mind the pre-emptive "response" to Black Lives Matters protests and other movements for social justice.

That's when Jesus rides in on the back of a donkey, accompanied by his followers: poor people, working-class folks, women, social outcasts. It was a direct action against the occupying forces, a rejection of the status quo. It was an in-your-face mockery. Yes, it was nonviolent, but it was also aggressive.

There is a clip in the documentary *How To Survive A Plague* of news footage from the early 1990s. AIDS activists have unveiled a sprawling quilt on the National Mall honoring those who have died from AIDS. When it was first unveiled, it contained 1,920 panels and covered a space larger than a football field. By this time in 1992, it had more than 21,00 handmade panels—greater than 10 times its original size.

On October 11, 1992, a large and scrappy group of people living with AIDS, queer people, friends, lovers, parents, and grandparents, marched to the White House lawn. With them, they carried the ashes of loved ones they lost to the plague.

"Bring the dead to your door! / We won't take it anymore!"

"Act up! Fight back! Fight AIDS! Act up! Fight back! Fight AIDS!"

"Shame! Shame! Shame!"

There's a clip in the news footage of survivors throwing the ashes of those they lost on to the White House lawn as they chant and scream and wail their names.

"I love you Mike! I love you Mike!" you can hear a man in his mid-thirties say as he tosses Mike's ashes through the fence.[2]

THAT is what the Palm Sunday procession was like. Defiant and hopeful and heartbroken. Peasants powerful enough to send shockwaves that still reverberate two millennia later.

Palm Sunday, like the Student Non-Violent Coordinating Committee lunch counter sit-ins before it in the 1960s and countless actions after it, were protests, yes, but they are also invitations:

(1) John Dominic Crossan and Marcus Borg, The Last Week
(2) to see video footage from this march, go to queertheology.com/ashes-action

"Which procession do you want to be part of?"

The Kingdom of Empire, which promises "peace" through military might, through the hoarding of resources, through the protection of the rich and powerful? Or the Kingdom of God, which promises freedom, justice, mercy, and enough for all?

That question is as alive and relevant as ever.

When we hold these stories together, then and now, something powerful happens. Our understanding of Palm Sunday comes to life in rich new ways and the meaning of current struggles is reinvigorated with an ancient, holy connection.

So which is it, Pilate's procession or Christ's?

Do we march in military and police parades? Do we line up behind the banks at Pride? Do we sit in the pews of the religious right who collaborate with a deadly and corrupt American empire?

Or do we take to the streets with Black Lives Matter? With Occupy Wall Street? With abolitionists and conscientious objectors and peace activists? Do we hoard what we have or do we share it?

The answer is important because, as Jesus demonstrates later that week, the answer can have costly consequences.

Journal Prompts

- ❖ How does thinking about Palm Sunday as a protest march change your understanding of it?
- ❖ What Palm Sunday moment is happening right now for you?
- ❖ What are the risks & costs, power & reward of joining the processional?
- ❖ What changes might you make to your life in response to this story?

Action Items

- ❖ Watch *How To Survive A Plague*.
- ❖ Attend a meeting of ACT-UP, VOCAL, Black Lives Matter, an indigenous rights protest, Showing Up For Racial Justice, The Coalition to Stop Gun Violence, or aother justice-oriented cause.
- ❖ Find & Attend a nonviolence / civil disobedience training.

Day Ten
A Depressed Prophet

If you have time, read 1 KINGS 19 in your favorite Bible translation then come back to this page.

If you're short on time, read this and pay attention to what jumps out at you as you read:

> *Elijah was terrified. He got up and ran for his life. He arrived at Beersheba in Judah and left his assistant there. He, himself, went farther on into the desert, a day's journey. He finally sat down under a solitary broom bush. He longed for his own death: "It's more than enough, Lord! Take my life because I'm no better than my ancestors." He lay down and slept under the solitary broom bush.*
>
> **1 Kings 19:3-5**

LGBTQ+ PEOPLE ARE 2 ½ TIMES MORE LIKELY to experience depression, anxiety, and substance misuse compared with heterosexual people[1], while we are 2 - 13 times more likely to have considered attempting suicide[2]. Even among straight, cisgender people, mental health issues are significant: over 16% of Americans have at least one major depressive episode in any given year[3].

It's not that being LGBTQ+ is a mental illness or that there's something inherently sick with us, rather it's that this world is a tough place, and it's even tougher for LGBTQ+ people.

Elijah understands a thing or two about that.

Here he is, one of the great prophets of the Hebrew Bible, and we find him holed up in a dark cave, buried under covers, too depressed to leave, wanting to die. Depressed and contemplating suicide. If that's ever been you, take notice: you are a part of the story of God's people too.

The messenger comes to help Elijah out of his depressive rut. How the messenger does so is instructive. The messenger doesn't tell him to shrug it off, that it's no big deal, that it's not real. The messenger doesn't tell Elijah, "God never gives you more than you can handle," or, "God has a reason for everything you experience." The messenger doesn't offer to pray for Elijah.

Instead, the messenger offers some practical advice: Get up. Go eat something.

Elijah goes out and looks for God's help in the rushing wind, in the trembling earthquake, in the blazing fire. But God wasn't there.

God was in the still small voice. The causes for mental illness and mental health struggles are varied and the appropriate treatments are too. More often than not, they aren't big gestures, but rather they begin with simple actions:

- Take a shower.
- Eat some soup.
- Take your medicine.
- Get some sunlight.
- Talk to your therapist.

When you are having a depressive bout or a burst of mania or near-crippling anxiety or dysphoria or a PTSD flashback or a psychotic break, you may feel like you don't fit in, that God has forsaken you or that you aren't valued. That's just not true.

Sometimes, the work to get well is tough. Sometimes, we feel "better" and sometimes we just learn how to manage and get by. You don't have to be perfect. Not for God, not for your community, not for anyone. All you have to be is human. All you have to be is you.

So lay down when you need to, and then, eventually, it will be time for you to get up, have something to eat, and try again.

---

(1) Kates, J, et al. "Health and Access To Care And Coverage For Lesbian, Gay, Bisexual, and Transgender Individuals in the U.S. Retrieved." KaiserFamily Foundation. 2016. http://kff.org/report-section/health-and-access-to-care-and-coverage-for-lesbian-gay-bisexual-and-transgender-healthchallenges/

(2) Mass. Dept. of Public Health, 2009

(3) https://www.healthline.com/health/depression/facts-statistics-infographic

Journal Prompts

- Have you experienced a time of depression? What was it like? What brought you out of it?
- What are the things that are most helpful to you when you are having a mental health crisis?
- What is keeping you from seeking help to better your mental health?

Actions

- Make a list of activities to feed your body, mind, and spirit that are easy to do, that you can turn to when times get rough.
- Buy some yummy, nourishing, non-perishable foods to have on-hand when you're too tired or stressed or depressed to figure out food: maybe some dried fruits, nuts, or a frozen dinner.
- God does not always speak to us in prayer or worship or through a sermon. Spend some time this week in activities where you might hear God's voice and feel God's presence: make art, go for a walk through nature, go for a walk through the city, practice yoga, take a dance class, sit in stillness, go out dancing and pay attention when you are in the middle of the dance floor.
- Take the day off. Rest. Sleep. Disconnect your devices. And then begin again tomorrow. ("Get up! Eat something," as the messenger told Elijah)

Day Eleven
Jesus Still Had His Scars

If you have time, read JOHN 20:19-29 in your favorite Bible translation then come back to this page.

If you're short on time, read this and pay attention to what jumps out at you as you read:

> *After eight days, his disciples were again in a house, and Thomas was with them. Even though the doors were locked, Jesus entered and stood among them. He said, "Peace be with you." Then he said to Thomas, "Put your finger here. Look at my hands. Put your hand into my side. No more disbelief. Believe!" Thomas responded to Jesus, "My Lord and my God!" Jesus replied, "Do you believe because you see me? Happy are those who don't see and yet believe."*
>
> **John 20:26-29**

IN THE CHURCH OF MY CHILDHOOD whenever this passage was preached on, the focus was always on Thomas's doubt. How could Thomas still doubt after all he had seen Jesus do? This then translated into an admonition about how we needed to be better than Thomas.

But reading this passage as an adult, I was struck by something totally different: Jesus's resurrected body. Jesus still has the scars from his horrific and brutal execution by the state. Even in his resurrected body, even in his Divine self, he is still carrying the scars of the wounds he received.

This moment of realization made me think about my own body and my relationship to my own scars: the one on my knee from when I wiped out on my bike going down a giant hill as a kid, the one that's so faint in my eyebrow from an encounter with a door as a toddler, and, of course, the scars that stretch across my chest from my chest-reconstruction surgery. I carry these scars with me everywhere I go. They are reminders of moments in my life, some of them pleasant, some not so much.

And then there are the invisible scars I carry: rejection from family and friends, religious trauma, and others. These, too, are scars that are healed but still leave a mark.

Jesus's body still having his scars taught me I don't have to try to make my scars go away. It's not about making sure every wound I have heals over and disappears. Instead, it's about making peace with scars and allowing their presence to continue to draw me closer to the miraculous: the miracles of my own body's and soul's healing power, the miracle of how far I have come, the miracle of all that I have survived.

Our scars aren't necessarily something to be healed; they are reminders of our encounters with the holiness of healing and the wonder of survival.

Journal Prompts

- ❖ What does thinking about Jesus still having his scars in his resurrected body do for you?
- ❖ What does it mean for you to think of your scars as holy?
- ❖ How can you forgive yourself for your moment of unbelief?

Action Items

- ❖ Spend some time reflecting on your scars. Light a candle, rub your scars with lotion, give thanks for the way your body heals.
- ❖ If you can, make a donation to a transgender person's surgery fundraiser.
- ❖ Make a list of all of the things you have a hard time believing. Try to make peace with the not knowing today.

Day Twelve
Fight For Your Faith

If you have time, read GENESIS 32 in your favorite Bible translation then come back to this page.

If you're short on time, read this and pay attention to what jumps out at you as you read:

> *But Jacob stayed apart by himself, and a man wrestled with him until dawn broke. When the man saw that he couldn't defeat Jacob, he grabbed Jacob's thigh and tore a muscle in Jacob's thigh as he wrestled with him. The man said, "Let me go because the dawn is breaking." But Jacob said, "I won't let you go until you bless me." He said to Jacob, "What's your name?" and he said, "Jacob." Then he said, "Your name won't be Jacob any longer, but Israel, because you struggled with God and with men and won." Jacob also asked and said, "Tell me your name." But he said, "Why do you ask for my name?" and he blessed Jacob there. Jacob named the place Peniel, "because I've seen God face-to-face, and my life has been saved." The sun rose as Jacob passed Penuel, limping because of his thigh. Therefore, Israelites don't eat the tendon attached to the thigh muscle to this day, because he grabbed Jacob's thigh muscle at the tendon.*
>
> **Genesis 32: 24-32**

JACOB IS NOT THE MOST LIKEABLE BIBLE CHARACTER. He's a trickster. He's willing to say and do just about anything to get what he wants. He looks out for himself and will take what he thinks he deserves. At least that's the picture that we get from a surface reading of the text.

If we go deeper, we find that Jacob is out of step with the men in his family. He prefers to stay in the kitchen with his mom, and he's derided for it. He knows that he's not going to get the biggest portion of his inheritance; whatever life he's going to make for himself he's going to have to work and fight for. And work he does. He works for his inheritance, for his wives, for his cattle. He lies and cheats, but he builds himself a life.

And then, when the life he wanted is built, he feels like he needs to make some things right, to go back home and make amends. He's nervous because he knows that his brother is probably still pissed, and when they parted there were threats made. He prepares himself as best he can, does what he can to protect his family and his fortune, and then goes off by himself.

A being appears to him, and they wrestle through the night. This man, no stranger to fighting for what he wants, refuses to let go. He demands a blessing. And once again he gets what he wants. Once again there is a cost for getting what he wants.

He comes out of this fight changed and with a new name. How many queer and trans folks know this story in our very bones? We know what it is to fight and wrestle. We know what it is to ask for a blessing. We know what it means to change our name.

Note that the text doesn't condemn Jacob for not letting go. It doesn't condemn him for wrestling or even for demanding a blessing. So hang on. Fight for your faith. Fight for your place. Demand that blessing.

Journal Prompts:

- When in your life have you wrestled with God? What happened?
- What would it feel like to demand a blessing from God?
- If God were to change your name, what do you think God would change it to?

Action items:

- Think about an issue you've been avoiding in your life. What might you do to tackle it and start dealing with it today?
- Find one thing to do today that would be a blessing to someone else.
- What is one thing you could do today to tenaciously push the world toward more justice?

Day Thirteen
The Body of Christ Has AIDS

If you have time, read 1 CORINTHIANS 12:1-31 in your favorite Bible translation then come back to this page.

If you're short on time, read this and pay attention to what jumps out at you as you read:

> *Just as a body, though one, has many parts, but all its many parts form one body, so it is with Christ. For we were all baptized by one Spirit so as to form one body—whether Jews or Gentiles, slave or free—and we were all given the one Spirit to drink. Even so the body is not made up of one part but of many. Now if the foot should say, "Because I am not a hand, I do not belong to the body," it would not for that reason stop being part of the body.*
>
> *But in fact God has placed the parts in the body, every one of them, just as he wanted them to be. If they were all one part, where would the body be? As it is, there are many parts, but one body.*
>
> *The eye cannot say to the hand, "I don't need you!" And the head cannot say to the feet, "I don't need you!" On the contrary, those parts of the body that seem to be weaker are indispensable, and the parts that we think are less honorable we treat with special honor. And the parts that are unpresentable are treated with special modesty, while our presentable parts need no special treatment. But God has put the body together, giving greater honor to the parts that lacked it.*
>
> *If one part suffers, every part suffers with it; if one part is honored, every part rejoices with it. Now you are the body of Christ, and each one of you is a part of it.*
>
> **1 Corinthians 12:12-15, 18-24, 26-27**

PAUL WAS A BIT OBSESSED WITH BODIES and his maladjusted relationship with them.

In his second letter to the Corinthians, he complains about the "thorn in his side." There was something about Paul that made him deeply uncomfortable with himself. Some scholars think that perhaps Paul was repressing his homosexuality. Of course, we can't know that for sure. In this passage, Paul talks about bodies again. And he's talking about genitalia.

"Those parts of the body that seem to be weaker," "the parts that we think are less honorable," "the parts that are unpresentable" ... he's talking about our genitals.

There are a number of different lessons you could take away from this text, all of them pretty queer.

It's got something to teach us about bodies, specifically:

Though culture tells us we are supposed to be ashamed of our bodies — too fat, too skinny, too sexual, not muscular enough, dirty, broken, disabled, Black, Brown, transgender, othered—whatever it might be—our bodies are good and holy, just the way they are. They couldn't be any other way, we need every body.

You don't have to be ashamed of parts of your bodies — the parts you use for sex or for breastfeeding or for going to the bathroom, or for any combination of the above. Those are good and honorable, too.

And this passage has something to teach us about the Body of Christ too:

There are lots of different ways to be part of the Body of Christ: wisdom and prophecy, knowledge and truth-telling. Some people are preachers, others are cooks, others manage the money to support the work. We need them all! You have something important to offer in the way you show up to yourself, your family, your community, your friend group, or your church.

But I want to take a moment and dwell at the intersection of our physical bodies and the more spiritual "Body of Christ."

We see in this passage, "We were all baptized by one Spirit so as to form one body," and that "if one part suffers, every part suffers with it." And so, when we look at the reality that members of the body of Christ are living with HIV/AIDS, we can only come to one conclusion:

The Body of Christ has AIDS.

For as long as there are people living with HIV/AIDS and suffering because of it, Christ, and all of us who belong in Christ, have AIDS as well.

For as long as there are people living with HIV/AIDS and thriving with it, finding blessed communities in it, Christ, and all of us who belong in Christ, have AIDS as well.

In this way, HIV/AIDS is both a suffering and an honor. It is a chronic health condition requiring diligent management. It is a pandemic which has been shamefully ignored, neglected, and sometimes even fueled by an uncaring public and discriminatory government, aided and abetted by Christians who traded grace for judgment. And so Christ is there, in the struggle.

For many Christians, the power of Christ's blood is a powerful symbol. If the Body of Christ has AIDS, then the holy, cleansing, powerful blood of Christ also has AIDS. The "blood that washes away sin" has AIDS. The "Blood of the Lamb" has AIDS. Blood with HIV/AIDS isn't dirty or shameful, it is given a place of honor.

We are all one body, and we need each other to survive.

Journal Prompts:

◆ What parts of your body are you ashamed of? How can you reframe that? What have those parts taught you? What is their power?

If you are living with HIV/AIDS:

◆ What are some lies others have told you about yourself, your body, and your blood—or that you have told yourself? What is the truth, instead?

◆ What role do you play in "the body" of your family, friend group, or faith community?

◆ How does thinking about the body and blood of Christ having AIDS change your relationship to it, to yourself, and to people who are HIV negative?

If you are HIV negative:

◆ What assumptions do you hold about people living with HIV/AIDS? What might you do to learn the truths instead?

◆ How does thinking about the body and blood of Christ having AIDS change your relationship to it and to people living with HIV/AIDS?

Action items:

◆ Spend 10 minutes in prayer or meditation. Lightly touch your foot, or focus your attention on it, and say to yourself "My body is good." Repeat this, working up your body: your knees, your legs, your butt, your crotch, your stomach, every body part up to the top of your head.

◆ Watch *Tongues Untied*, *We Were Here*, or *How To Survive A Plague*.

◆ Most gay and bisexual men are unable to donate blood. Write to government officials who represent you and ask them to pressure their party to make revising the FDA guidelines a priority.

◆ Donate blood, if you can. Tell friends and family about the blood ban.

Day Fourteen
Christ's Temptation, Our Liberation

If you have time, read LUKE 4 in your favorite Bible translation then come back to this page.

If you're short on time, read this and pay attention to what jumps out at you as you read:

> *The devil brought him [Jesus] into Jerusalem and stood him at the highest point of the temple. He said to him, "Since you are God's Son, throw yourself down from here; for it's written: He will command his angels concerning you, to protect you, and they will take you up in their hands so that you won't hit your foot on a stone." Jesus answered, "It's been said, Don't test the Lord your God." After finishing every temptation, the devil departed from him until the next opportunity.*
>
> *Jesus returned in the power of the Spirit to Galilee, and news about him spread throughout the whole countryside. He taught in their synagogues and was praised by everyone. Jesus went to Nazareth, where he had been raised. On the Sabbath, he went to the synagogue as he normally did and stood up to read. The synagogue assistant gave him the scroll from the prophet Isaiah. He unrolled the scroll and found the place where it was written:*
>
>> *The Spirit of the Lord is upon me,*
>>   *because the Lord has anointed me.*
>> *He has sent me to preach good news to the poor,*
>>   *to proclaim release to the prisoners*
>>   *and recovery of sight to the blind,*
>>   *to liberate the oppressed,*
>>   *and to proclaim the year of the Lord's favor.*
>
> **Luke 4:9-19**

THE BEGINNING OF JESUS'S MINISTRY is a series of what seem like disconnected stories: First he's baptized by his cousin and hears a voice from heaven calling him beloved. Then we read Jesus's genealogy. Then he's led into the wilderness where he faces a series of temptations. Then it's back to the synagogue where he reads from the scroll and teaches for the first time.

What is going on here?

The author of Luke is telling those reading what kind of ministry Jesus is being called to. First, the author makes sure that we know that something different happens when John baptizes Jesus. This isn't just another baptism, but a sign from Heaven that says to pay attention. Then the author connects Jesus's lineage to David and to Adam showing that he's part of the kingly line, part of the ruling class and community. But then the author pushes Jesus into the wilderness. And the temptations Jesus is subjected to are specific: they are about power and control. They are about feeding himself (the role of the emperor), about taking power over the land he could see, and about protecting himself above all else. And in each case, Jesus rejects the temptation.

Then, finally, he reads from the prophet Isaiah and tells us his mission: to release prisoners, heal the sick, liberate the oppressed, and proclaim the jubilee (an economically motivated statement)! Jesus has been given the chance to take hold of kingly power. We're even told that it would be his birthright! Instead he chooses to serve, to take on the mantle of a prophet.

In doing so, he calls those of us who follow him to do the same, to look at the ways we can work for liberation instead of the ways we can gain more power. Jesus's ministry was never about theological saving but about the real, concrete, liberation of people.

Journal Prompts:

- What does this passage teach us about the kind of ministry Jesus feels called to?
- What temptations have you faced when it comes to following in the way of Jesus?
- Where are the places in your life where oppression still has a grip on you?

Action items:

- Check out Black and Pink and see about becoming a penpal with an LGBTQ person in the prison system. Or check out one of the many book projects that work to get reading materials to people in prison.
- Look for a place to volunteer in your community: maybe it's working at a food pantry or with a street outreach team. Find some way to alleviate the suffering of people who are financially insecure.
- Thinking about the journaling prompt about oppression above, what are some actions you can take to alleviate the oppression you are under?

Day Fifteen
Family

If you have time, read MARK 3:20-35 in your favorite Bible translation then come back to this page.

If you're short on time, read this and pay attention to what jumps out at you as you read:

> *[Jesus's] mother and brothers arrived. They stood outside and sent word to him, calling for him. A crowd was seated around him, and those sent to him said, "Look, your mother, brothers, and sisters are outside looking for you." He replied, "Who is my mother? Who are my brothers?" Looking around at those seated around him in a circle, he said, "Look, here are my mother and my brothers. Whoever does God's will is my brother, sister, and mother."*
>
> **Mark 3: 31-35**

THERE ARE VERY FEW MENTIONS OF JESUS'S FAMILY OF ORIGIN in the Gospels. The Gospel of Mark, especially, since it has no birth narrative, is short on details. In this passage we see that people are starting to grumble about Jesus. They're saying that he's possessed, they are watching him closely, and into this mix comes his mother and brothers and sisters.

We don't know why Jesus's family comes to see him. Maybe they had heard the stories circulating and came to warn him, maybe they wanted to tell him to stop all of this nonsense and come home, maybe they wanted to join in the movement. The text doesn't really tell us because Jesus refuses to see them.

We also don't know why Jesus refused to see them. Maybe they had already had fraught conversations about his work and ministry, and he knew this was going to be more of the same. Maybe he was feeling particularly fragile that day and knew if they asked him to go home he would. Maybe he was simply trying to make a point to the people around him.

No matter the reason, as queer and trans folks, I think we feel this passage intimately. Even if our families are affirming, they've often done hurtful things on their journey toward that affirmation, or said something unintentionally hurtful. Or maybe they are not affirming at all. In this passage we see Jesus giving us two wonderful examples: the ability to set boundaries, even with our own families, in order to protect ourselves, and the gathering around of a chosen family who understands and supports you unconditionally.

Journal Prompts:

- Have you ever felt alienated from your family of origin? What was that like?
- Do you have people in your life that you consider your family? Who are they? What do they mean to you?
- What does it mean to you that Jesus felt alienation from his family of origin? What does it mean that he gathered around him people who he felt comfortable with?

Action items:

- Write a note to someone in your chosen family and thank them for playing a supportive role in your life.
- Write a note to someone who has acted as a surrogate parent or mentor and thank them.
- Reach out to someone you think could use some support/community and let them know you are there for them.

Day Sixteen
Why Did Jesus Come?

If you have time, read JOHN 10:7-21 in your favorite Bible translation then come back to this page.

If you're short on time, read this and pay attention to what jumps out at you as you read:

> *"I came that they may have life and have it abundantly."*
> **John 10:10 (ESV)**

WHY DID JESUS COME? The Gospel of John offers one answer: so that we may have an abundant life.

Abundance has been twisted by some preachers and teachers to mean excess: a "prosperity gospel" that promises mansions and luxury cars and designer clothes and the latest trendy sports car... but somehow that only materializes for those in power.

The idea of abundance is found throughout the Hebrew and Christian Scriptures but this excess-called-abundance is not what the Biblical idea of abundance is.

Instead, here are just a few passages for reflection:

"God's love has been poured into our hearts through the Holy Spirit who has been given to us."
Romans 5:2-5

"God shows his love for us, because while we were still sinners Christ died for us."
Romans 5:8

"Give thanks to the God of heaven, for his steadfast love endures forever."
Psalm 136:26

"And God is able to make all grace abound to you, so that always having all sufficiency in everything, you may have an abundance for every good deed."
2 Corinthians 9:8

"I am the LORD your God, who brought you up out of the land of Egypt. Open your mouth wide, and I will fill it."
Psalm 81:10

"For he satisfies the thirsty and fills the hungry with good things."
Psalm 107:9

"You crown the year with your bounty; your wagon tracks overflow with abundance."
Psalm 65:11

We see throughout Scripture—from the Torah through the psalms and prophets and gospels to the letters of the early church—that God is concerned with us here and now. Our life is supposed to be full of abundant joy, not sorrow or misery, guilt or shame. Abundance is certainly not the same as "excess," but it's also not the same thing as "just barely enough." We aren't meant to just scrape by. When we are beaten down by the world around us, God mourns at a still-imperfect creation. God wants us to be able to let our guard down, to exhale, to breath easily.

"I came that they may have life and have it abundantly."

I came that they may have life and have it without fear of violence.

I came that they may have life and have it in a safe and stable home.

I came that they may have life and have more than enough to eat.

I came that they may have life and have it filled with joy.

I came that they may have life and have it filled with laughter.

I came that they may have life and have it in a body that is right for them.

It's a beautiful idea, but sometimes the disconnect between that holy vision and our grim reality can be depressing. If Christ came that we may have life and have it abundantly, why don't we? There are no simple answers, and there's no magic prayer to make it so. There's not a guarantee that anything will ever change. The kingdom of God is not yet on earth as it is in heaven. But we Christians believe that it can be. Jesus's earliest followers saw their leader tortured and executed by the State, and then a few days later something happened that resurrected their movement and filled them with an unstoppable vigor, an unshakeable faith in the mercy and abundance of God. They defied the most powerful empire in the world in their attempt to make it so.

Today, we pick up their work of making it so. And if today you can't, if today you are worn out and burnt out, disillusioned and disappointed, put down the load and rest today. Know that there are millions of LGBTQ+ Christians around the world working together with you and for you that you might experience abundant life.

Journal Prompts:

- ❖ What are some ways your life is already filled with abundance?
- ❖ What would it take to lighten your load a bit?
- ❖ Where would you like to experience more abudance?

Action items:

- ❖ At the end of each day, make a list of a few things for which you are grateful.
- ❖ Whenever something fulfilling or exciting happens, write it down on a notecard and place the card in a jar. At the end of the year, read through your collection of positive memories.
- ❖ Create a listing on Couchsurfing.com.
- ❖ Stop going to a church that doesn't affirm you.
- ❖ Donate to a GoFundMe.

Day Seventeen
Down But Not Destroyed

Read 2 CORINTHIANS 4:8-13 below or in your favorite Bible translation. Pay attention to what jumps out at you as you read.

> *We are experiencing all kinds of trouble, but we aren't crushed. We are confused, but we aren't depressed. We are harassed, but we aren't abandoned. We are knocked down, but we aren't knocked out.*
>
> *We always carry Jesus' death around in our bodies so that Jesus' life can also be seen in our bodies. We who are alive are always being handed over to death for Jesus' sake so that Jesus' life can also be seen in our bodies that are dying. So death is at work in us, but life is at work in you.*
>
> *We have the same faithful spirit as what is written in scripture: I had faith, and so I spoke. We also have faith, and so we also speak.*
>
> **2 Corinthians 4:8-13**

THE STORY OF THE EARLIEST CHRISTIANS was one of resilience. They faced persecution from the occupying Roman empire and misunderstanding from many within the Jewish community, from whom they were splitting away. Resilience is the story of the LGBTQ+ community, too. Sometimes we face outright hostility, while other times we face a more subtle judgement or misunderstanding. (Of course, we also experience joy and acceptance and jubilation!)

This passage from 2 Corinthians could be speaking to us.

We experience trouble, but we aren't defeated by it.

We are confused, but we keep going.

We are harassed, but we have each other's backs.

We are knocked down—physically & spiritually—but that can't stop us.

We aren't immortal or invincible though. Sometimes we are defeated, we are crushed, we are depressed, we are killed. That truth is reflected in this letter, too.

We are no stranger to death.

Nearly an entire generation of gay and bisexual men was killed by the early days of the AIDS epidemic. We carry death in our body.

The weight of an unaccepting and unaffirming society is sometimes too much to bear. Some in our community end their life in response. We carry death in our body.

Transgender people are disproportionality targeted and killed just for who they are. We refuse to accept that and we refuse to forget them, so we act and remember. We carry death in our body.

And yet...

We have that "faithful spirit." Have you been to a Pride parade? Have you been to a dyke march? Have you been to the trans day of action? Have you been to a queer support group? Have you been to a gay wedding? Have you been to a poly or kink munch? That indomitable spirit is in full display: love, joy, resilience, community, commitment.

We have seen the depths of the hard times and refused to be defeated because we know the heights of joy we can create together. We, like the earliest Christians, have always had faith in things unseen. "Another world is possible," they and we say.

When you come out... you had faith, and so you spoke.

When you talk to your doctor about transition... you had faith, and so you spoke.

When you sue your employer for discrimination... you had faith, and so you spoke.

When you form community and family in ways that are right for you... you had faith, and so you spoke.

That is what the LGBTQ+ community does: we also have faith, and so also we speak.

Journal Prompts:

- What about your life today at one point seemed impossible to you?
- What is a truth about yourself you are keeping inside? Whom could you speak that to?

Action Items

- Make an impossible list: a list of big, audacious dreams that seem impossible. Write them down. Maybe one day they'll come to be.
- Look up an LGBTQ-inclusive church in your area—or one that has a livestream or online community—and attend a service or small group. Don't know where to start? Join Sanctuary Collective.
- Transgender Day of Remembrance happens every year on November 20. Mark the date in your calendar and make a point to find a service to attend.

Day Eighteen
Doers Of The Word

If you have time, read JAMES 1:19-27 in your favorite Bible translation then come back to this page.

If you're short on time, read this and pay attention to what jumps out at you as you read:

> *You must be doers of the word and not only hearers who mislead themselves. Those who hear but don't do the word are like those who look at their faces in a mirror. They look at themselves, walk away, and immediately forget what they were like. But there are those who study the perfect law, the law of freedom, and continue to do it. They don't listen and then forget, but they put it into practice in their lives. They will be blessed in whatever they do. If those who claim devotion to God don't control what they say, they mislead themselves. Their devotion is worthless. True devotion, the kind that is pure and faultless before God the Father, is this: to care for orphans and widows in their difficulties and to keep the world from contaminating us.*
>
> **James 1:22-27**

I GREW UP IN A CHURCH that put a lot of emphasis on reading and memorizing the Bible. We spent a lot of time listening to sermons and talks and devotionals. There were a lot of speakers and teachers and preachers. And often, when we talked about the "doing" of our faith it was about spending MORE time reading and listening and learning. Sure, we were also supposed to work on our temper and not swear and all that stuff, but beyond that, it was about investment in the learning itself.

Then here comes the writer of James talking about pure devotion being caring for orphans and widows. True devotion means putting all of this reading and memorizing into concrete practice. And it's not really about your temper or your language, it's about caring for the most marginalized. When you do that, that's how you show devotion and keep the world from contaminating you.

It's not watching a sex scene in a movie or saying a "bad" word that contaminates you, it's conceding to a world that says that orphans and widows should be ignored. It's looking at church growth as simply numbers and butts in seats instead of on the impact that church has on the neighborhood: and not impact counted in church membership but impact counted in real, physical needs met!

If your faith isn't put into practice in the real world, then what good is it?

Journal Prompts

- ❖ What does it mean to be a "doer of the word"?
- ❖ What would it look like if you put your faith into practice?
- ❖ Where are the areas in your life where your belief and your practice are out of alignment?

Action Items

- ❖ What is one action you can take this week to put your faith into work in the world?
- ❖ Look up an organization in your area that cares for children or the elderly and find out how you can get involved.
- ❖ Work to bring your faith and practice into alignment in one of the areas where they are currently not.

Day Nineteen
Your Body Is A Temple

If you have time, read 1 CORINTHIANS 6:12-20 in your favorite Bible translation then come back to this page.

If you're short on time, read this and pay attention to what jumps out at you as you read:

> *Or don't you know that your body is a temple of the Holy Spirit who is in you? Don't you know that you have the Holy Spirit from God, and you don't belong to yourselves? You have been bought and paid for, so honor God with your body.*
>
> **1 Corinthians 6:19-20**

THIS IS ONE OF THOSE PASSAGES that is sometimes used against LGBTQ+ people (and women and anyone desiring sexual or bodily autonomy). "Your body is a temple, don't transition." "Your body is a temple, don't have sex." "Your body is a temple, it is not your own."

Nonsense.

Your body is a temple, be grateful for it.

Your body is a temple, take care of it.

Your body is a temple, worship with it.

Your body is a temple, enjoy it.

At the start of this section, the writer says, "I have the freedom to do anything." How often do you hear that?

In Christ, we have freedom. This doesn't mean our actions don't have consequences. For the verse goes on to say, "but not everything is helpful."

What is helpful for you?

Are hormones or surgery or new clothes helpful for you? Do that.

Is masturbation helpful for you? Do that.

Is sex helpful for you? Do that.

We can't ignore that this passage talks about sexual immorality. What is that? Not some laundry list of dos and don'ts but rather anything that separates us from each other and from God. "Love your neighbor as yourself," remember.

When it comes to sexuality, love your neighbor or your spouse or your lover or the person you just met online as yourself.

This passage also talks of two becoming one flesh. Here it says, "Don't you know that anyone who is joined to someone who is sleeping around is one body with that person? The scripture says, The two will become one flesh."

I couldn't agree more. In fact, I'd take it a step further. I think this goes beyond just sex in the way we normally understand it. I carry bits and pieces of my first boyfriend Ben around with me, even though all we ever did was kiss and hold hands. Parts of him are "stuck" to me like lint on tape.

When we are intimate with someone — through sex or love or both — we become a bit like them, they are imprinted on us in ways big and small. So who we are intimate with matters. There isn't a list of "right" or "wrong" acts to do or avoid. Instead, remember that your body is a temple, invite those in who will honor and respect it. You deserve it.

Journal Prompts

- In what ways have you neglected your body?
- How can you honor your body more?
- Who are some people you still carry around in your heart? What did you learn from them? What do they add to your life — and thus the body of Christ?

Action Items

- Write a letter of gratitude to someone you've been intimate with (you don't need to send it, but you can).
- Start each morning with some mantras affirming the goodness of yourself and your body. Need some inspiration? Take a look at queertheology.com/morning-mantras

Day Twenty
Reaping The Harvest

If you have time, read PSLAM 126 in your favorite Bible translation then come back to this page.

If you're short on time, read this and pay attention to what jumps out at you as you read:

> *Lord, change our circumstances for the better,*
> *   like dry streams in the desert waste!*
> *Let those who plant with tears*
> *   reap the harvest with joyful shouts.*
> *Let those who go out,*
> *   crying and carrying their seed,*
> *   come home with joyful shouts,*
> *   carrying bales of grain!*
>
> **Psalm 126 4-6**

THERE HAVE BEEN TIMES IN MY LIFE WHEN I THOUGHT EVERYTHING WAS OVER. Times of great grief and distress: a relationship ending, leaving a church, coming out and losing friends. The list goes on. In those moments of grief, it can be hard to think about anything else.

And yet, I also know, looking back on those times from the distance of years and healing, I can see something amazing grew from those experiences. I love this line in the Psalm: "Let those who plan with tears reap the harvest with joyful shouts."

Lines like this aren't meant to glorify suffering. It's not saying that we need to be thankful for bad things that happen to us, or gloss over harm done to us because, "God will bring something good out of it." But it is a reminder that sometimes pain does bring growth. Sometimes the ending of a relationship makes space for a new one to flourish. Sometimes leaving a church means that you can find health and healing. Sometimes coming out means you lose one community only to find another where you can be yourself.

This cry of the Psalmist for God to bring about a harvest of joy can be your cry, too.

Journal Prompts

- ❖ Are there moments in your life where the seeds of grief grew something beautiful?
- ❖ Is there something in your life that is currently causing you pain? Can you take a moment to sit with and honor your grief?

Action Items

- ❖ Do something tangible to honor/remember a time of grief in your life.
- ❖ Do something in memory of someone who has died that would honor them.
- ❖ Spend some time in prayer today asking God to help you change the circumstances in your life where you are unhappy. Then take one concrete action to move with God.

Day Twenty-One
I Am A Sodomite

If you have time, read GENESIS 19:1-28 and EZEKIEL 16:49-50 in your favorite Bible translation then come back to this page.

If you're short on time, read this and pay attention to what jumps out at you as you read:

> *"Now this was the sin of your sister Sodom: She and her daughters were arrogant, overfed and unconcerned; they did not help the poor and needy. They were haughty and did detestable things before me. Therefore I did away with them as you have seen."*
>
> **Ezekiel 16:49-50 (NIV)**

I AM A REFORMED SODOMITE.

Not because I stopped having gay sex (I still do that!) but because of the Biblical meaning of the word Sodomite.

It is true that for at least a century, "sodomite" has been used as a slur against gay men. It is equally true that there is no compelling Biblical justification for that.

That's not what our focus is today, though. Instead, this is a moment to ask, "What is a sodomite?" And how are we convicted by that?

Scripture itself spells out exactly what the sin of Sodom was: arrogance, excess, neglect. There was a time when that could have easily described me. There are times if I do not guard my heart when arrogance, excess, or neglect can creep in or spill out.

For those of us who are LGBTQ+ Christians, it can be tempting to re-read the story of Sodom and Gomorrah and confidently proclaim: THAT'S NOT ABOUT US!

But it might be. Not because the story of the destruction of Sodom and Gomorrah might be about a condemnation of LGBTQ+ experiences (it most definitely is not), but because even LGBTQ+ people can be arrogant, excessive, or neglectful. In focusing on how Sodom and Gomorrah isn't about homosexuality, we miss an important opportunity for conviction and growth.

I'm a proud homosexual, but I'm a repentant Sodomite.

Journal Prompts

- In what areas of my life am I arrogant, inhospitable, greedy, or neglectful? In what areas is my community arrogant, inhospitable, greedy, or neglectful?
- How does it feel to release any argument about homosexuality with respect to this passage and instead focus on (in)justice?
- What do I feel—in my body—when I consider that I might be convicted by this passage? What could that teach me?

Action Items

- Make a habit to donate regularly to your local food bank.
- Give directly to people in need in your neighborhood or on your streets.
- Write, call, or visit your elected officials and ask them to do more to support people who are homeless, elderly, living in poverty, or living with disabilities.

Day Twenty-Two
Come and See

If you have time, read JOHN 1:31-51 in your favorite Bible translation then come back to this page.

If you're short on time, read this and pay attention to what jumps out at you as you read:

> *The next day John was standing again with two of his disciples. When he saw Jesus walking along he said, "Look! The Lamb of God!" The two disciples heard what he said, and they followed Jesus. When Jesus turned and saw them following, he asked, "What are you looking for?" They said, "Rabbi (which is translated Teacher), where are you staying?" He replied, "Come and see." So they went and saw where he was staying, and they remained with him that day. It was about four o'clock in the afternoon.*
>
> **John 1:35-39**

WE OFTEN THINK OF "EVANGELISM" AS THE HARD SELL. Going up to strangers on the street and telling them about Jesus. We get visions of John the Baptist on the street corner screaming for people to "Repent!" Jesus is presented as doing something completely different. In this story, Jesus waits until someone approaches him. When he notices that people are watching and interested, he asks them a question, "What are you looking for?" It's a striking question with a lot of layers. It can be answered in so many different ways. Jesus had this way of getting to the heart of things.

The people following choose to answer the question on a surface level; they want to know where Jesus is staying. And once again, Jesus answers in a profound way, "Come and see."

Jesus could have answered their question differently. He could have railed at them for the way they answered his question, "What are you looking for?" He could have said, "Don't you know I was asking you to examine your hearts, not just asking a surface-y question?"

He could have answered by saying, "Oh, I'm staying on such and such street" and then gone on his way. He could have even led them to where he was staying and pointed it out and then gone inside on his own. Instead he did something more than that, he invited them to "come and see" and then, when they got there, he invited them to come inside and spend the day with him.

Jesus waits for an opportunity: he doesn't just go up to a stranger-the people were following him already. Jesus asks a question that cuts to the heart of their lives and is centered on their needs. What are you looking for? Are you looking for hope? Are you looking for peace? Are you looking to be involved in something that gives you meaning? Are you looking for community? What are you looking for?

Then Jesus invites them to come and see. He is doing more than just inviting them to come over to his house; he is inviting them to see who he is and how he lives. He's inviting them to see how his message brings liberation in actual lives. But here's the real kicker: he had something for them to see. And what he had for them to see was so compelling that they gave up everything and followed him.

We can learn a lot from Jesus's methods about what it means to tell people about our faith and about the goodness of trans and queer lives. This idea of sharing the Good News of God with people is something that needs to be done in a way that is natural to you. It needs to be done in the context of a relationship. It's as simple as saying, "Come and see."

Journal Prompts

- ❖ Do you struggle with talking about your faith with other people? What about your identity?
- ❖ If you could easily share with other people, what would you want them to know about your faith and your life?
- ❖ What does Jesus's statement "come and see" mean to you?

Action Items

- ❖ Who might you invite into your life to "come and see" this week?
- ❖ Share one thing about your identity with someone close to you.
- ❖ Share a way you are growing in your faith with someone in your life.

Day Twenty-Three
Word Became Flesh

Read the following verses below or in your favorite Bible translation. Pay attention to what jumps out at you as you read.

And the word became flesh and dwelt among us.

John 1:14

I will ask the Father, and He will give you another Helper, that He may be with you forever; that is the Spirit of truth, whom the world cannot receive, because it does not see Him or know Him, but you know Him because He abides with you and will be in you.

John 14:16-17

When Pentecost Day arrived, they were all together in one place. Suddenly a sound from heaven like the howling of a fierce wind filled the entire house where they were sitting. They saw what seemed to be individual flames of fire alighting on each one of them. They were all filled with the Holy Spirit and began to speak in other languages as the Spirit enabled them to speak.

Acts 2:1-4

JOHN'S ACCOUNT OF THE GOSPEL BEGINS with the word of God becoming flesh and dwelling among us. This is a common theme among the Gospel writers and has always been central to the Christian tradition: God among us. Emmanuel. This is not an "out there" religion, it is embodied.

Later in John's Gospel, the writer recounts Jesus telling his followers that though Jesus's time is limited, a spirit of truth—a spirit of God—is available to all of us. That spirit will dwell inside of us. In our bodies.

And then, of course, in the Acts of the Apostles, we have the famous story of Pentecost. The Holy Spirit descends and fills all who are gathered: a bunch of holy flamers.

While the Gospel of John begins with the word of God becoming flesh in the person of Jesus, Jesus's ministry ends with a proclamation that the spirit of God is to be enfleshed in each of us. Acts recounts a grand occurrence of just that.

God isn't just somewhere in heaven, God was here on earth in Jesus, and God is here still in you, in me, in us.

That changes everything.

Jesus was an unlikely person for his followers to claim as Son of God. Caesar was supposed to be the Son of God—rich, powerful, violent—not some homeless, traveling, Jewish peasant.

The crowd gathered at Pentecost could have been accused of insurrection. "If they are good guys, they should stay home. Anyone outside is a criminal. That's why the police have to shoot them." The charges leveled against protestors today could have been made against them, too.

To follow Jesus was to be an outlaw. Not because they selfishly refused to bake cakes for gay couples and had nondiscrimination laws equally applied to them, like some faux-martyrs today pretend; rather, it was a radical love and hospitality. It was a renunciation of violence and division. It was grace and humility that made those early Christians outlaws.

Queer people know a thing or two about being outlaws. For much of modern history, our existence was illegal (and still is for many people around the world).

But still, we gathered. Genderbenders and gays, trans folks, lesbians and bisexuals. Butches and sissies and faggots and pansies and poofters. At bars and clubs and private living rooms and public parks. An outlaw gathering of holy flamers, much like those earliest Christians at Pentecost.

The Spirit still moves among us, wherever we are gathered.

Sometimes when I'm at a gay club, I take a step back and watch my friends shower each other with physical affection. Hugs and kisses and winks and nods and silly faces and pinched cheeks and grinding and making out.

If you squint your eyes just right, you can see the Holy Spirit.

Where might God be that you have missed out on?

Journal Prompts

- What unexpected places have you encountered the divine?
- Where else might God be that you have missed out?
- What changes for you when God is not somewhere out there but in each of us?

Action Items

- Try out a spiritual practice to pay attention to the divine voice inside of you. Need some inspiration? We have some ideas + instructions at queertheology.com/spiritual-practices.
- Go to a queer cafe, gay club, or LGBTQ+ bookstore and look to see and feel how the Holy Spirit is present there.
- Show up for someone in a time of need—physically go be with them.

Day Twenty-Four
Offer Your Body

If you have time, read ROMANS 12 in your favorite Bible translation then come back to this page.

If you're short on time, read this and pay attention to what jumps out at you as you read:

> *Therefore, I urge you, brothers and sisters, in view of God's mercy, to offer your bodies as a living sacrifice, holy and pleasing to God—this is your true and proper worship.*
>
> **Romans 12:1 (NIV)**

WHEN YOU THINK OF WORSHIP, what comes to mind?

Music? Instruments? Singing? Perhaps raised hands or closed eyes or quiet reflection?

Paul, in his letter to the Romans, imagines worship as something quite different: embodied.

What does it mean to offer your body as a sacrifice? Here is what I think of:

AIDS activists who chained their bodies together inside of pharmaceutical headquarters to demand the life-saving medications their community so desperately needed.

Freedom Riders who put their bodies on buses into the south to undermine white supremacy, some of whom sacrificed their lives, too.

Indigenous communities standing on their ancient and hallowed ground, using their bodies to try to stop the Dakota Access Pipeline at Standing Rock or the Trump speech at Six Grandfathers Mountain (also known as Mount Rushmore) in the Black Hills.

But I don't only think of protest when I think of offering our bodies as a living sacrifice. I think of my queer family showing up with our bodies to sit beside our friend in the hospital as he undergoes surgery after surgery to keep his terminal cancer at bay.

I think about the deep care and consideration transgender people give to their bodies and how they intentionally, painstakingly, oftentimes at great cost use their bodies to express their inner divinity.

I think of queer couples—and triads and moresomes—who brought their bodies together and danced at bars and loved in bedrooms (and backrooms) when doing so was illegal.

A few years ago, I went over to the apartment of a guy I'd hooked up with a few times before. This was supposed to be a quick fling. He met me at the door and silently escorted me to his bedroom and we began to have sex. But something just wasn't right. The physical logistics weren't lining up quite right and we had to take a pause. And in that pause, I realized there was something more going on. I leaned forward and kissed him, and pulled him sideways so that we flopped down on the bed next to each other, naked and intertwined.

"What's wrong?" I asked.

"I can't start talking about it or I won't stop crying," he replied.

So we sat in silence for a few moments and then he began to tell me about the boy who was breaking his heart. And then, like he said he would, he started crying. And I held him and kissed his cheek gently and ran my fingers through his hair as he choked back the tears and continued to tell the story.

We laid there, our bodies laid bare as physical offerings to each other as he bared his heart and I received it. And when he had let the weight go from his chest and the tears dried from his eyes, we laid there some more as the afternoon sun streaked across our chests and warmed our skin. And then it was time to go; him to a grad-school class, me back to my home office. I pulled up my jeans as he pulled on his sweatpants, and we walked down the rusty New York City stairs and out into the warm autumn afternoon and kissed goodbye one last time before parting ways.

This is all true and proper worship.

Journal Prompts

- What does worship look like to you?
- What do you already do that seems "secular" or even "profane" that you might think about differently as worship?
- What is a time that you experienced the presence of God? Describe it it in detail.

Action Items

- Give a friend, partner, lover, or parent a massage.
- Attend a protest.
- Go out dancing with friends, bring an intention of worship with you.

Day Twenty-Five
What Are You Building On?

If you have time, read Luke 6:39-49 in your favorite Bible translation then come back to this page.

If you're short on time, read this and pay attention to what jumps out at you as you read:

> *"Why do you call me 'Lord, Lord' and don't do what I say? I'll show what it's like when someone comes to me, hears my words, and puts them into practice. It's like a person building a house by digging deep and laying the foundation on bedrock. When the flood came, the rising water smashed against that house, but the water couldn't shake the house because it was well built. But those who don't put into practice what they hear are like a person who built a house without a foundation. The floodwater smashed against it and it collapsed instantly. It was completely destroyed."*
>
> **Luke 6:46-49**

Shortly after college, I was reading *Stealing Jesus* by Bruce Bawer. It's a book about how certain evangelical beliefs came into being, especially in the United States. As I read along I got to a section on the rapture where the author reveals that an English guy named Darby came up with this idea about 150 years ago. Wait. WHAT?!?! This idea that had caused so much fear in my body growing up was only 150 years old? My church had taught it as if Jesus himself had handed down this teaching. I began to wonder what else I hadn't been told.

The faith of my youth was built like a house of cards. Everything depended on everything else. If you pulled a card, the entire thing came crashing down. It's like this house Jesus is talking about in Luke, the one that's built on sand. One firm wave comes and the whole thing gets knocked down.

It's why so many of us got obsessed with coming up with a good answer to the "Clobber verses", determined to build a strong defense. We kept chasing better and stronger defenses, wondering why we never felt really secure. After months or maybe even years we learned the entire idea of the clobber passages was built on sand.

What is your faith's foundation? What do you know for sure? Start there and then build. But don't be afraid to re-evaluate if you find that something you once thought was rock turns out to be sand.

Journal Prompts

- ❖ What are you building the foundation of your faith on?
- ❖ Journal about a time when you felt your faith shift because your foundation got rocked. What did that teach you?
- ❖ What is one thing that feels rock-solid to you in your faith life/belief system?

Action Items

- ❖ Make a list of beliefs you feel confident in that you can turn back to when you feel battered by life's storms.
- ❖ Make a list of the teachers/people in your life you know you can trust to tell you the truth.
- ❖ Do one thing this week that affirms the faith journey you've been on.

Day Twenty-Six
Fire In My Bones

If you have time, read JEREMIAH 20:7-18 in your favorite Bible translation then come back to this page.

If you're short on time, read this and pay attention to what jumps out at you as you read:

> *Within me there is something like a burning fire*
> *shut up in my bones;*
> *I am weary with holding it in,*
> *and I cannot.*
>
> **Jeremiah 20:9b (NRSV)**

JEREMIAH LOOKED AT THE WORLD AROUND HIM and was compelled to speak. He saw violence and destruction and knew that this was not the way it was supposed to be. There was a conviction in his heart and to stifle it felt impossible.

This passage from Jeremiah has both a pastoral and a prophetic message. Jeremiah was a prophet and so the context of this text is him speaking truth to power. He witnessed the excesses and inequalities of his community and felt compelled to speak out. That cost him. The priest, Pashhur, had him arrested, possibly whipped, and placed in stocks for mockery and judgment. Still, Jeremiah was undeterred.

> *For whenever I speak, I must cry out,*
> *I must shout, "Violence and destruction!"*

It is our call to be like Jeremiah, unable to remain silent in the face of injustice. To speak the truth of divine justice, even when it is costly.

This passage can also have a pastoral message for you, too. There are truths inside of you burning like a fire, shut up in your bones. Truths that are causing you to grow weary by all the efforts you make to suppress them.

Maybe this is an inclination about the reality of your gender. Maybe it is a mental illness or disability that you work hard to mask. Maybe it's the truth about how you love. Maybe it is a growing realization that you are not home in your family of origin.

Whatever it is, listen to it. It has something to teach you, even if it is scary.

As you pay attention to what your body and soul are telling you about yourself, as you speak that truth, you will be transformed. The more you pay attention to the fire in your bones about yourself, the greater you will be able to pay attention to the fire in your bones about the world around you. As you speak a prophetic, liberating word about the world around you, you may awaken to new truths about yourself. This is a cycle that repeats and reinforces. "Love your neighbor as yourself," with a bit more fiery oomph!

Sometimes, we do not even realize the load we carry. We have become so used to being weary that we mistake it for normal. We might even think this is how everyone feels. If there is something within you like a burning fire, you don't have to keep it shut up. You don't have to be brought down by it. On the other side is liberation. It may not always be pleasant—sometimes you may find yourself in the stocks, like Jeremiah—but it is worth it.

Speak the truth that is burning inside of you.

Journal Prompts

- ◈ What truths about yourself are you holding in?
- ◈ What truths about the community and world around you are holding back?
- ◈ How do you *feel*, in your body?

Action Items

- ◈ Write down something you've been scared to say to others. If you are scared others will see it, you can throw it away or shred it or burn it or rip it into tiny pieces and drop them in different trash cans.
- ◈ Say a scary truth out loud. Wait until you are home alone or go find a quiet place outside. If you feel up for it, tell one person: a friend, a social media connection, you can even send us an audio message on Instagram.
- ◈ Write a letter to a lawmaker who represents you about an issue important to you. Even if you don't have a proposed solution, tell them why it's important to you and what you hope to see.
- ◈ Attend a rally in your city for a social justice cause that matters to you.

Day Twenty-Seven
The One That Was Tossed Aside

If you have time, read 1 PETER 2 in your favorite Bible translation then come back to this page.

If you're short on time, read this and pay attention to what jumps out at you as you read:

> *Now to you who believe, this stone is precious. But to those who do not believe,*
>
> > *"The stone the builders rejected*
> > *has become the cornerstone,"*
>
> *And, "A stone that causes people to stumble and a rock that makes them fall." They stumble because they disobey the message—which is also what they were destined for. But you are a chosen people, a royal priesthood, a holy nation, God's special possession, that you may declare the praises of him who called you out of darkness into his wonderful light. Once you were not a people, but now you are the people of God; once you had not received mercy, but now you have received mercy.*
>
> **1 Peter 2:7-10**

WHEN I READ THESE VERSES about "the stone that the builders tossed aside," my mind immediately goes to queer and trans people of faith. How often have we been pushed or tossed aside? How often have our needs been considered irrelevant? How many times have we been told we are too divisive, or to wait a little longer, or that we are simply not welcome at all? We've heard this from our churches, our families of origin, our countries. We hear it on the news and on the internet.

And yet the very next piece is that the stone that was rejected has become the cornerstone. The stone on which everything else rests. Our rejected identities become the place of strength, the place of building, the foundation. And the people who refuse to believe, who continue to reject us, they are the ones who stumble and fall. They are the ones who miss out on all of the goodness that is here with us.

Once you weren't a people, but now you are God's people. Every time we build queer community every time we look out for one another, we're building this. As we remember all we've been through to get here and continue to work for more justice and more security, we just keep remembering we are God's people. We are God's people and the strength of the foundation rests with us.

Journal Prompts

- ❖ What does it feel like to think of your queerness/transness as something vital for Christian community?
- ❖ How has your faith grown since you acknowledged and accepted your identity?
- ❖ What does it feel like to hear "But you are a chosen race, a royal priesthood, a holy nation, a people who are God's own possession," as relating to your orientation or gender identity?

Action Items

- ❖ Do something to honor your identity today.
- ❖ Shar e one insight that you have learned because of your identity that might benefit others.

Day Twenty-Eight
Honoring Marriage & Family

If you have time, read Hebrews 13:1-16 in your favorite Bible translation then come back to this page.

If you're short on time read this and pay attention to what jumps out at you as you read:

> *Keep loving each other like family. Don't neglect to open up your homes to guests, because by doing this some have been hosts to angels without knowing it. Remember prisoners as if you were in prison with them, and people who are mistreated as if you were in their place. Marriage must be honored in every respect, with no cheating on the relationship, because God will judge the sexually immoral person and the person who commits adultery. Your way of life should be free from the love of money, and you should be content with what you have. After all, he has said, I will never leave you or abandon you. This is why we can confidently say,*
>
> *The Lord is my helper,*
>   *and I won't be afraid.*
> *What can people do to me?*

Hebrews 13:1-6

THERE ARE SOME PASSAGES THAT HAVE QUEERNESS LURKING JUST BELOW THE SURFACE if you'll just look for it. Hebrews 13 is one such passage.

The early church was a group of people bound by similar experiences, united together under a common mission and identity. They came from different backgrounds — some Jewish, some Gentile; some old, some young; some rich, some poor; some from high standing, some without title or even home; all different genders and languages and cultures. In the beginning, Christians were an oppressed minority but the growing community was numerous enough that they didn't all know each other; they hadn't all met. Much of their connection was through letters and traveling teachers.

That describes the LGBTQ+ community just as much as it does the early church, doesn't it?

Many of our families of origin don't support us like they should, and so chosen family is a deep tradition in the queer community. When you read "Keep loving each other like family" in this passage, that is a call for chosen family!

LGBTQ+ people know a thing or two about that. We "keep loving each other like family." Those of us in cities open up our homes to LGBTQ+ folks fleeing their homes to find safe haven in the city. Those of us in the suburbs and rural areas open up our homes to the newly out (or the newly outed) so they don't have to flee in the first place.

Do you know of a single LGBTQ+ person who hasn't crashed on a friend's couch or hosted a friend (or a stranger) for a night or a week or longer?

The Bible has been wielded against LGBTQ+ people so often that when we see "marriage," many people assume that means "straight, cisgender marriage." Surely when the writer of Hebrews was putting this letter together, it's doubtful he was imagining modern queer couples. But that doesn't make us any less present.

"Marriage must be honored in every respect, with no cheating on the relationship" is a value LGBTQ+ Christians can rally behind, too.

Now, no person is perfect and neither is any community. Infidelity is part of the human experience and it knows no gender, sexuality, religion, or region. But taking relationships seriously? LGBTQ+ people have that in spades. For much of modern history, our relationships have been deemed sick, sinful, perverted, and illegal.

There's a sepia-toned photograph of two young men in 1900 holding a small sign between them that says "Not married but willing to be!"[1] Queer people have been taking marriage seriously for centuries, millennia even. You can see in the glint of their eyes that even though their relationship would be illegal for another century, they know the pure joy and holiness of it.

LGBTQ+ people form relationships in all sorts of different ways: legal marriage, civil or social partnership, queer platonic friendships, blended families, lesbians and gay men having children together, polyamory, relationship anarchy, a blurred line between friend and lover, the list could go on for pages. What is common in all of those is that we take relationships seriously. We have to. Our lives depend on it.

LGBTQ+ people don't end up in relationships by accident, we choose them because they matter to us. We take them seriously. How much more seriously can you take commitment in relationships than to pursue it in the face of a society conspiring against you?

(1) See the photo at queertheology.com/queer-marriage-photo

For centuries, LGBTQ+ people have risked our lives for our marriages and relationships. We've developed our own ceremonies to honor them when the world around us woldn't. We've fought for every single piece of religious and legal marriage that we have.

This passage doesn't say "Marriage must be heterosexual" or even "Marriage must be monogamous." Instead, it says to take marriage seriously. It says to honor your commitment to your partner (or your partners).

Queer people form families not because it's what is expected of us or by accident but my choice and with serious intention. Our families are not just those to whom we are related by blood but include those forged together through mission and community. THAT is taking marriage and family seriously. Thus, queer relationships and chosen family are an ultimate expression of divine community.

Journal Prompts

- ◆ If you are LGBTQ, what is something that your straight, cisgender friends and family can learn from the way you approach relationships?
- ◆ If you are straight & cisgender, what is something that you have learned about relationships from the LGBTQ+ people in your life?

Action Items

- ◆ If you are in a relationship, spend some time with your partner to explicitly articulate your commitments to one another, whatever stage or form of relationship you are in. Write them down.
- ◆ Tell your friends you love them.
- ◆ Host a dinner party. If you're feeling bold, invite your friends to invite a friend of theirs you don't know (yet).
- ◆ Take a QueerTheology.com online workshops on Faithful Sexuality or Christianity & Polyamory to learn more about how queer sex and relationships reflects the divine.

Day Twenty-Nine
Community

Read HEBREWS 10:22 - 25 below or in your favorite Bible translation then come back to this page.

> *And let us consider each other carefully for the purpose of sparking love and good deeds. Don't stop meeting together with other believers, which some people have gotten into the habit of doing. Instead, encourage each other, especially as you see the day drawing near.*
> **Hebrews 10:22-25**

STAYING IN COMMUNITY IS TOUGH.

It's easier to cut and run rather than face uncomfortable truths. Sometimes, it's easier to brush off a slur hurled from a stranger than to hear from a close friend that something we did or said hurt them.

We've done a disservice to Christianity by turning it into a system of personal piety. Jesus taught his disciples to pray for "our daily bread." He taught them to ask that God's will be done all over the earth. He called his followers to be the salt of the earth and to let their light shine.

A private Christianity is understandable.

For too long, an aggressive, militaristic, sexist, homophobic version has reigned supreme in the modern public sphere. It has been used to gut social services for the most vulnerable in our society, to start never-ending wars, to undermine women's control over their own bodies. Heck, Christianity was used as a justification to steal the land the United States of America now claims through a coast-to-coast genocide.

No wonder, in reaction to that type of Christianity, we want to isolate religion to a matter of personal beliefs that have no bearing on our public behavior.

But the Gospel is supposed to be good news for all people. Even for those who don't believe in it or want to follow it.

Our faith must be communal.

Matthew 18:20 says

> *"Where two or more are gathered in my name, there I am."*

We are in this together.

The beauty of grace is that the discomfort doesn't need to last. The apostle Paul went from a persecutor of early believers to arguably the most influential evangelist. Community keeps you accountable, but community also is there to celebrate with you as you grow and transform.

That doesn't happen when you sit alone on your couch and binge the latest reality show on your favorite streaming service. At some point, we must each peek out from behind our book or podcast or computer and interact with other people, people who have their own personalities and needs and ideas and feelings. People whom we may hurt or be hurt by.

But, as it says in this passage, "Let's draw near with a genuine heart with the certainty that our faith gives us." "Let's hold on to the confession of our hope without wavering." "Let us consider each other carefully."

Community is absolutely worth it. It's how LGBTQ+ people have survived and thrived for so long.

We are in this together.

We have an opportunity to let our faith be good news to a world in need, but we can't do it alone. We can't feed the hungry, clothe the naked, and set free the prisoners alone. The early church in Acts shared everything they had in common... you can't share by yourself.

Find community.

Create community.

Cherish community.

Allow yourself to be transformed by community.

Journal Prompts

- Who is part of your community?
- How have you been helped by your community? How have you been hurt by it?
- How have you helped your community? How have you neglected it?
- "Community" can mean many things — friends, a network of people connected by some identity like religion or sexuality, or the community of your physical space. Which type(s) of community do you feel most connected to? How could you cultivate connections in other communities you are not already part of?

Action Items

- Call a friend and tell them what they mean to you.
- Pay attention to your friends' moods and needs. Do something kind and helpful for them, without them asking.
- Host a dinner party or game night (in real life or virtually) for your friends or community.

Day Thirty
God's Good News

If you have time, read Isaiah 61 in your favorite Bible translation then come back to this page.

If you're short on time, read this and pay attention to what jumps out at you as you read:

> *The Lord God's spirit is upon me,*
>   *because the Lord has anointed me.*
> *He has sent me*
>   *to bring good news to the poor,*
>   *to bind up the brokenhearted,*
>   *to proclaim release for captives,*
>   *and liberation for prisoners,*
>   *to proclaim the year of the Lord's favor*
>   *and a day of vindication for our God,*
>   *to comfort all who mourn,*

Isaiah 61:1-2

When we talk at QueerTheology.com about there being an arc of justice to Scripture, this passage from Isaiah is one of the things we're talking about. Not only does it have a clear call toward justice, but it's this passage that Jesus reads in the synagogue in Luke 4 when he starts his public ministry.

When Jesus picks up that scroll and reads, he is saying, "I'm here to fulfill this. This emphasis that has always been part of our tradition? I'm here to remind you of it and make it happen." It's not about supplanting the Hebrew Scriptures, but about calling us back to the heart of the message. Justice.

If we're ever to think of the Bible as a list of do's and don'ts, the focus of that list isn't about what to read or watch or say. It's not even about whom to avoid having sex with. It's about this: good news for the poor, release of the prisoners, declaring the year of jubilee (which was an erasing of debt).

What would it look like in your life if that were the list of principles guiding you? What would it look like if our churches took that list seriously? How would it change things?

Journal Prompts

- What would it change in your faith if you believed the arc of Scripture was toward justice?
- How are you involved in work for justice in your community?
- How is your church/friend group/community working for justice?

Action Items

- Do one thing to bring good news to people who are financially insecure today.
- Do one thing to support someone in prison.
- Do one thing to help erase someone's debt.

Day Thirty-One
Rest

If you have time, read MATTHEW 11:1-10, 28-30 in your favorite Bible translation then come back to this page.

If you're short on time, read this and pay attention to what jumps out at you as you read:

> *Come to me, all you who are weary and burdened, and I will give you rest. Take my yoke upon you and learn from me, for I am gentle and humble in heart, and you will find rest for your souls. For my yoke is easy and my burden is light."*
>
> **Matthew 11:28**

THERE IS A LOT TO DO.

LGBTQ+ Christians are often acutely aware that we live in an unjust world. Routine, even comforting, activities for straight, cisgender people can be hurdles we must clear.

Will this preacher say something anti-queer?

Can we get legally married?

Will we be allowed to adopt?

Will the doctor honor our wishes about our partner's healthcare?

We can take nothing for granted.

And so many of us, out of necessity, have become educators and activists: with our doctors, with our pastors, with our parents, with our employers.

The experience of discrimination in our personal lives can open us up to the injustice others, who are not like us, face. From there, a sacred solidarity can form. It really is inspiring.

John the Baptist and Jesus knew a thing or two about this. They were living as Jews under Roman occupation. There was always something for them to do, too. "Prepare ye the way!" as the musical Godspell tells it. Action is central to the gospel message.

It's important to remember, though, that we are only human. Humans whom God cares about very deeply. We cannot keep up an endless cycle of "go go go."

There is always another hard conversation to have, meeting to organize, rally to attend.

If visiting your family leaves you feeling drained...

If you spend hours on the phone with doctors and insurance agents and more doctors and therapists because simple healthcare has become a never-ending series of hurdles...

If you bristle at some point during every sermon because of something the pastor said...

If you've lost track of the number of times you've talked to HR about co-workers who won't call you by your name and pronouns...

God is calling you.

Come and rest in the embrace of God's love for you.

Rest.

This isn't to say that you should give up and accept mistreatment but it is a reminder that you are worthy of rest. It's allowed to be easy.

It's ok to leave the church.

It's ok to call in sick.

It's ok hang up the phone and relax with a book and delicious food.

It's ok to spend less time witih people who don't see, understand, and affirm you and more time with friend and chosen family who do.

It's ok to stop going home.

Sometimes, remembering that God's yoke is easy and God's burden is light means simply stopping. Stop. Stop doing the thing that is getting you down. Let it be easy.

Sometimes, though, there are forces bearing down on us that we can't control. In those times, remember you are not alone. You are not the first to go through this trial. Yes, of course, God is there too. But that can be cold comfort when faced with the harshness of reality. There are other people—real, living, breathing, feeling people—who have been there too. Or who haven't been there but want to support you nonetheless.

Rivers ramble because they go where the earth gives way with the least resistance. The course of a river doesn't change drastically overnight; instead, it changes slowly over time, little by little, day by day, following this easier course. A little movement today, a little more movement tomorrow. Still more movement after that until you've found the river of your life has snaked around the obstacles and cleared a path to something new.

That is the invitation of this teaching: to keep moving, yes, but to do so in the places where it is easy. There is no glory to be found in making it harder or heavier than it needs to be.

Jesus calls out to those who "weary and burdened." Is that you? If so, put down your burdens, the yoke of Jesus should lighten you not weigh you down.

Remember to rest.

Journal Prompts

- ◈ In what ways have you made following God a burden? What would it mean for you to lighten that load?
- ◈ Where do you feel stuck?

Action Items

- ◈ Take a nap.
- ◈ Call a friend and ask for help.
- ◈ Pick something to stop doing.

Day Thirty-Two
The Wicked & The Righteous

If you have time, read MATTHEW 25:31-46 in your favorite Bible translation then come back to this page.

If you're short on time read this and pay attention to what jumps out at you as you read:

> *"Then the king will reply to them, 'I assure you that when you have done it for one of the least of these brothers and sisters of mine, you have done it for me.'*
>
> *"Then he will say to those on his left, 'Get away from me, you who will receive terrible things. Go into the unending fire that has been prepared for the devil and his angels. I was hungry and you didn't give me food to eat. I was thirsty and you didn't give me anything to drink. I was a stranger and you didn't welcome me. I was naked and you didn't give me clothes to wear. I was sick and in prison, and you didn't visit me.'*
>
> *"Then they will reply, 'Lord, when did we see you hungry or thirsty or a stranger or naked or sick or in prison and didn't do anything to help you?' Then he will answer, 'I assure you that when you haven't done it for one of the least of these, you haven't done it for me.' And they will go away into eternal punishment. But the righteous ones will go into eternal life.*
>
> **Matthew 25:40-46**

IF YOUR AVERAGE STREET PREACHER OR PRIDE PROTESTOR is any indication, the Gospel is more bad news than good news: fire and hell and damnation.

It's true that in parts of the Bible, the writers talk about fiery pits or eternal damnation (though, it's not nearly as common as you may think, look it up!). This passage from Matthew is one such place.

Here, Jesus is telling a story about the wicked and the righteous and the fates that await them both. LGBTQ+ people are used to being cast as "the wicked" in stories about sin or sickness. Maybe you've been told that who you are or how you love or what you do with your body is wrong. Maybe you've been told that you are in danger of judgment and damnation. It's the rare queer person who makes it through life without being told to "Repent!" at least once.

Jesus here is quite clear about who receives judgement and punishment. Who is it? What do you read? Those who do not feed hungry and thirsty people, those who do not help strangers and people living in prison and people who have been incarcerated. That sounds an awful lot like the ones doing all of the condemning on TV and in the street and even sometimes from the pulpit.

Even still, if LGBTQ+ people are not the object of Jesus's ire here, isn't this still a portrait of a judgmental and violent God? "Eternal punishment"? Does God damn people to hell? What about "love wins"?

In the story here, it's God who is separating the metaphoric sheep from the goats, casting those of who take care of each other to one side and those of who neglect and abuse to the other side. Do we really need to be sorted, though? Perhaps, rather than a literal king-on-high doing the sorting, this is a story reminding us of exactly the way things are.

When we ignore those in need and are complicit in others' imprisonment, we cut ourselves off from our shared humanity. You may not notice it at first—or ever—but you are cut off from the source of life. The divine is found in each and every person. Each and every person! We must all be connected to each other in order to be connected to the source of life.

You may have experienced this: when you find and form family and community that truly, fully embrace and care for each other. When you learn across culture and experience deep connection with people who are different from you. Jesus and his followers weren't waxing poetic about theology from their armchairs or their seminary classrooms or their laptops: they were out in the world. Traveling. Experiencing. Healing. Liberating. It's not about saying the right words or believing the right things. It is about action. It is about embodiment.

This passage in Matthew calls us to step out into the world and do something about it. Not out of fear of judgment some day in the future, but rather because each day we don't, we continue to torment ourselves eternally. And when we do, when we experience that connection, we understand what it means to have everlasting life because we taste it here and now.

Journal Prompts

- Who are the "least of these" in your day to day life?
- Do you think that you are a sheep or a goat? If you don't like your answer, how might you change it?
- Have you ever had an experience where you feel like Jesus "visited you" in the form of another person? What happened? How did it make you feel?

Action Items

- Donate to your local food bank—or give money directly to someone asking for it
- Get involved with prison abolition work through an organization like Black & Pink or Critical Resistance
- Donate to an LGBTQ homeless shelter
- Contact your local lawmakers to share your support for funding for people in need of homes
- Watch *13* by director Ava DuVernay

Day Thirty-Three
Jesus Comes Out

If you have time, read MATTHEW 17:1-13 in your favorite Bible translation then come back to this page.

If you're short on time, read this and pay attention to what jumps out at you as you read:

> *While he was still speaking, look, a bright cloud overshadowed them. A voice from the cloud said, "This is my Son whom I dearly love. I am very pleased with him. Listen to him!" Hearing this, the disciples fell on their faces, filled with awe. But Jesus came and touched them. "Get up," he said, "Don't be afraid." When they looked up, they saw no one except Jesus.*
>
> **Matthew 17:5-8**

IN THIS PASSAGE, JESUS DOES SOMETHING VERY FAMILIAR for many queer and transgender people: he pulls aside his closest friends, takes them off to a place where they can speak privately, and he reveals something about his identity to them that they didn't know about before. Call it Jesus's coming out moment; the Transfiguration marked a new phase in the life of Jesus and his ministry.

Coming out can be scary. Coming out isn't a once-and-done event. Every time we meet someone new or start a new job or move to a new place, the process begins again. Even if we are out and proud it can still be exhausting. We worry we'll be rejected (or worse). We get tired of explaining our identity to other people.

And yet, every time we come out it's an opportunity for a deeper connection with the people we are coming out to. It's a moment we get to reveal part of ourselves to another person and become more intimate with them. When we come out, we create opportunities for people to say: "This is my friend in whom I am well pleased."

Journal Prompts

- What does it do for you to think of Jesus needing to "come out" about a part of his identity?
- What have your various coming out experiences been like (even if you're only out to yourself)?
- How has coming out increased intimacy with other people in your life?

Action Items

- Write a note of encouragement to someone who isn't out yet. Maybe this takes the form of a letter posted on your Facebook page or with a photo on Instagram. Share how coming out has impacted your life.
- Write a letter to your closeted self and tell them all the things you know now that you didn't know then.
- Find someone safe in your life to have a deep conversation with, revealing something new about yourself.

Day Thirty-Four
Shake Them Off & Leave Them Behind

If you have time, read MATTHEW 10:5-15, MARK 6:1-13 and/or LUKE 10:1-24 in your favorite Bible translation then come back to this page.

If you're short on time, read this and pay attention to what jumps out at you as you read:

> *Jesus said to them, "A prophet is not without honor except in his own town, among his relatives and in his own home."*
>
> **Mark 6:4**

> *If any place will not welcome you or listen to you, leave that place and shake the dust off your feet as a testimony against them.*
>
> **Mark 6:11**

EVERY SINGLE PERSON has the capacity to love, affirm, and cherish LGBTQ+ people. Not everyone will.

You cannot control another person. You cannot make them love or accept you. You cannot make them use your correct name and pronouns. You cannot make them attend your wedding or commitment ceremony.

All you can do is invite them to listen to the good news of your life that you have to share with them.

Some people are ready to welcome you in and have already prepared a feast for you. Some people will be wary and have questions and reservations but will be willing to talk and listen with an open mind. Others won't.

There will be people in your life who, as Jesus warns, "will not welcome you or listen to you." They might open the door but not welcome you in. They might even ask questions, but are they truly listening to your response?

Many LGBTQ+ Christians and straight, cisgender supporters feel an obligation to "stay and fight," to change the hearts and minds of their congregation or their family. But that's not what Jesus is instructing here.

If they will not listen to you, it is not your job to stay and fight, it's your responsibility to shake the dust off of your sandals and move on.

There are others out there who WILL welcome you, who DO want to listen to you, who NEED the message you have to share. Every minute you spend banging your head against a wall is a minute that could be spent—but is not—in pursuits that lead to life.

This is not an admission of defeat nor a judgment upon the hearts of those you leave behind, it is only a recognition of reality: we only have so much time on this planet, how we spend it matters.

So spend it wisely.

Journal Prompts

- ❖ When have you shared an important truth that was well-received? How did that feel?
- ❖ Who is someone who didn't initially understand or agree with LGBTQ+ people/issues but, through your conversations together, learned and grew? Who is someone who stayed stuck in their beliefs? How did you feel about each?
- ❖ What is the difference between the two? How can you tell?
- ❖ What would it feel like if you spent almost all of your time talking with people who wanted to listen, learn, and grow?

Action Items

- ❖ Make a list of people & organizations who don't affirm you and haven't demonstrated any willingness to learn or grow. Make a plan for "shaking the dust off" of your sandals.
- ❖ Make a list of people who love and support you plus those who don't understand but want to learn and grow. Make a plan to spend more time with them.
- ❖ If you want to be around people willing to learn and grow, join Sanctuary Collective.

Day Thirty-Five
With His Body

If you have time, read EPHESIANS 2:11-22 in your favorite Bible translation then come back to this page.

If you're short on time read this and pay attention to what jumps out at you as you read:

> *Christ is our peace. He made both Jews and Gentiles into one group. With his body, he broke down the barrier of hatred that divided us. He canceled the detailed rules of the Law so that he could create one new person out of the two groups, making peace. He reconciled them both as one body to God by the cross, which ended the hostility to God. When he came, he announced the good news of peace to you who were far away from God and to those who were near.*
>
> **Ephesians 2:14-16**

THROUGHOUT SCRIPTURE, over and over again, the Bible talks about unity. It can sometimes seem like this emphasis on unity is all about blending, smoothing over differences, ignoring identities. Instead, when we read these passages, we should be reminded that it's not about the flattening of identities, it's about a justice orientation that works to overcome the systems that make some identities "worth more" than others.

The idea of peace is central to the Scriptures, but it's always centered in justice. Chants of "No justice, no peace" could have come from the Psalms. In this message to the Ephesians, Paul talks about how Jesus brought about peace "with his body."

With his body, he broke down the barriers of hatred. He put his body on the line to speak truth to power. He put his body on the line to center the marginalized. He put his body on the line to bring about justice.

If we want to follow in the way of Jesus, it's not about our assent to creeds, it's not fluffy unity at all costs, it's about where our bodies are. It's about working for justice with our actions. That's how we both honor a diversity of identities and carry on the mission Jesus started.

Journal Prompts

- What does working for justice with your body mean to you?
- How does this reframing of the work of Jesus resonate with you?
- Whom do you need to stand in solidarity with?

Action Items

- What is one action you can take this week to put your body into the work for justice?
- Search out and listen to a voice from a community that is not your own, then take the action they are asking you to take.

Day Thirty-Six
What God Has Made Clean

If you have time, read ACTS 10 in your favorite Bible translation then come back to this page.

If you're short on time read this and pay attention to what jumps out at you as you read:

> *At noon on the following day, as their journey brought them close to the city, Peter went up on the roof to pray. He became hungry and wanted to eat. While others were preparing the meal, he had a visionary experience. He saw heaven opened up and something like a large linen sheet being lowered to the earth by its four corners. Inside the sheet were all kinds of four-legged animals, reptiles, and wild birds. A voice told him, "Get up, Peter! Kill and eat!" Peter exclaimed, "Absolutely not, Lord! I have never eaten anything impure or unclean." The voice spoke a second time, "Never consider unclean what God has made pure." This happened three times, then the object was suddenly pulled back into heaven.*
>
> **Acts 10: 9-16**

AFTER JESUS'S DEATH AND RESURRECTION, he basically left his followers to figure out how to continue without him. The disciples quickly stepped up as the leaders of the fledgling movement, but, as in all movements, questions of protocol, of inclusion, of organization quickly came to the forefront. In the beginning, the disciples' first priority was to people from within their community, other Jews. But throughout the book of Acts we see that priority being challenged and shifted. Two chapters prior we see Phillip baptize the Eunuch from Ethiopia, and now we have Peter having visions about what is clean and unclean.

Peter's vision repeats three times. The same amount of times he denies Jesus. The same amount of times Jesus asks Peter if he loves him. This repetition of three would have made quite the impact on Peter. At first he considers these visions a test and he's determined not to fail. Of course he's not going to eat unclean things! But the Spirit continues to push and finally says "Never consider unclean what God has made pure." And at that moment servants from a Gentile's household come and ask Peter to visit them.

To Peter's credit he goes. He changes his entire worldview. He not only preaches to them and baptizes the household, but he also eats with them and stays overnight in their house. The bounds of inclusion just got a little wider.

Sometimes people reject what they don't understand. Or they reject something because they are convinced they know what God thinks. But if we are still and quiet and really listen, we hear the Spirit continually challenging us to go further, to spread welcome wider, to stop considering things unclean.

Journal Prompts:

- ❖ What does Peter's change of mind teach you?
- ❖ Has there ever been a time when you've been completely convinced that something was correct only to have your viewpoint challenged? Did you change your mind? How did that feel?
- ❖ What groups of people does the church still consider "unclean"?

Action items:

- ❖ Find a group (doesn't have to be LGBTQ+) that is working for inclusion in the church and find out how you can get involved.
- ❖ Think about a group you consider "unclean" or you don't understand and read some first person narratives where people from that group share their stories.
- ❖ Do some research on how to have conversations with people who disagree with you. Make some notes about tactics that are helpful and try to incorporate them into your conversations.

Day Thirty-Seven
Come Alive, Dry Bones

If you have time, read EZEKIEL 37: 1-14 in your favorite Bible translation then come back to this page.

If you're short on time read this and pay attention to what jumps out at you as you read:

> He said to me, "Human-one, these bones are the entire house of Israel. They say, 'Our bones are dried up, and our hope has perished. We are completely finished.' So now, prophesy and say to them, 'The Lord God proclaims: I'm opening your graves! I will raise you up from your graves, my people, and I will bring you to Israel's fertile land. You will know that I am the Lord when I open your graves and raise you up from your graves, my people. I will put my breath in you, and you will live. I will plant you on your fertile land, and you will know that I am the Lord. I've spoken, and I will do it.' This is what the Lord says."
>
> **Ezekiel 37:11-14**

EZEKIEL IS A PROPHET, and like most prophets, he can be a little sarcastic. He's been called to minister to people who are going through an incredibly difficult time. They've been in exile for ages, away from their homeland, forced to find new and creative ways to keep their faith and their traditions alive. I'm sure many of them were losing hope. They thought their exile would be shorter than it was turning out to be, and now people were dying far, far away from home.

God brings Ezekiel to this valley of bones and asks him if the bones can live. One can forgive Ezekiel's snark as he says, basically, "Uh, hell if I know!" But God commands him to speak to the bones and call to the wind, and when he does the bones are resurrected. And now just the bones, but now they have flesh and muscle on them again. Fully restored. And God promises the same for the house of Israel.

For those of us who feel like we're in exile–estranged from our families or the church traditions of our youth, outcasts in our country or political system, longing to feel welcome and accepted–this passage can seem like cold comfort. Where is our promise? Where is our resurrection?

And yet, Ezekiel was commanded to play a part, to speak life to the bones, to call for help from the winds. Where are the places in your situation that you can speak life to? What is the wind that needs to blow through and bring something new? How can you call upon and nurture that wind for yourself or someone else today?

Journal Prompts

- ◈ What is feeling dead in you that you can speak life to?
- ◈ What are you feeling in exile from? What would it look and feel like to come back from exile?
- ◈ Where are the places in your life that you are feeling called to change?

Action Items

- ◈ Find something to nurture this week. Maybe it's spending time with an animal, repotting a plant, or reading a story to a child. Find something alive and offer some care.
- ◈ Reach out to someone in your life who's been having a hard time and speak a word of hope to them: something that might restore their faith or give them encouragement.
- ◈ What is one action you can take today to start to nurture the wind of change in your life?

Day Thirty-Eight
What Is Worship?

If you have time, read AMOS 5 in your favorite Bible translation then come back to this page.

If you're short on time read this and pay attention to what jumps out at you as you read:

> *"I hate, I despise your religious festivals;*
> *your assemblies are a stench to me.*
> *Even though you bring me burnt offerings and grain offerings,*
> *I will not accept them.*
> *Though you bring choice fellowship offerings,*
> *I will have no regard for them.*
> *Away with the noise of your songs!*
> *I will not listen to the music of your harps.*
> *But let justice roll on like a river,*
> *righteousness like a never-failing stream!*
>
> **Amos 5:21-24**

JEAN-MICHEL BASQUIAT once said,

"Art is how we decorate space, music is how we decorate time."

There is something ancient about music. We feel it in our bones and in our souls. The hum, the thump, the lift, the drop. Whether it's muzak in an elevator, a full orchestra at Lincoln Center, a DJ at an underground rave, or the choir at church, music does something to us. It connects us, grounds us, lifts us, inspires us, comforts us.

Music is a good thing,

It's no wonder, then, that music takes a central place in most churches. What that music sounds like and what those musicians look like varies greatly from church to church. For some, it's a centuries-old organ and a massive choir, for others it's a full rock band, complete with lights and fog and drums, for others it's a simple piano and a few enthusiastic, if slightly out-of-tune, volunteers.

Music is precious for churches, and it's easy to cast judgment upon how those other churches do their music. But that's not what Amos is getting at here. It's not that contemporary worship is more relevant or that hymns are more pure. It's that none of it matters if you aren't pursuing justice.

Worship isn't only about what you do on Sunday morning. It's about what you, together with your community, do every single day. A Christian music festival that fills an arena or the National Mall is noise if justice isn't rolling down. The sweet sound of your tiny church choir is caustic noise if justice isn't rolling down.

Worship is accessible bathrooms.

Worship is inclusive language.

Worship is protest marches.

Worship is food banks.

Worship is letter-writing campaigns.

Worship is hard conversations with friends, family, and neighbors.

Worship is prison abolition.

God's people have been using music to worship for millennia. Let music touch and transform you. Let it lift your spirit and move your heart… and then let it move your body out into the street until justice rolls down like a never-failing stream.

Journal Prompts

- ❖ What does "justice" mean to you?
- ❖ What and who inform your understanding of justice?
- ❖ Where is the disconnect between the values you express in worship and the ways your community/communities are structured? How can you begin to bridge the gap?

Action Items

- ❖ Make a list of priorities you see reflected in scripture, then find music that speaks to those priorities (you may need to search out some music that isn't considered "Christian")
- ❖ Pay attention to the lyrics of your favorite worship songs. Make a list of some ways you could embody the values of those songs.

Day Thirty-Nine
Spiritual Hunger

If you have time, read ACTS 8:26-40 in your favorite Bible translation then come back to this page.

If you're short on time read this and pay attention to what jumps out at you as you read:

> *Starting with that passage, Philip proclaimed the good news about Jesus to him. As they went down the road, they came to some water. The Eunuch said, "Look! Water! What would keep me from being baptized?" He ordered that the carriage halt. Both Philip and the Eunuch went down to the water, where Philip baptized him. When they came up out of the water, the Lord's Spirit suddenly took Philip away. The Eunuch never saw him again but went on his way rejoicing. Philip found himself in Azotus. He traveled through that area, preaching the good news in all the cities until he reached Caesarea.*
> **Acts 8:35-40**

THE FIRST GENTILE CONVERT to following the way of Jesus was a transgender person of color. Known as the Ethiopian Eunuch, the story in Acts 8 tells us of a person who feels a deep spiritual hunger but isn't sure how to express it. This person was coming home from the Temple. There's just one problem: as an outsider and as a Eunuch there's no way they would have been let inside to participate in worship ceremonies. And yet, they still feel a desire to connect with God.

Many queer and trans people know this experience intimately: a longing for spiritual community and practice but feeling rejected because of our sexual orientation or gender identity. What's incredibly powerful about this story is the dedication of the Eunuch to getting their needs met.

They continue to study on their own, even if they have trouble understanding. When an opportunity to connect with a mentor arrives, they take full advantage and ask lots of questions, and then, even though they know the odds are stacked against them, they ask for entry into this new community and their boldness is rewarded.

The Ethiopian Eunuch teaches us to strive to meet our spiritual needs however we can, to take advantage of opportunities to learn and to grow, and to be bold in pushing churches not just to tolerate us but to fully affirm and celebrate our lives.

Journal Prompts

- ❖ Can you think of a time in your life when you felt a deep, spiritual hunger? Write about it.
- ❖ Journal about a time when you felt rejected from a place you deeply wanted to belong. What did you learn from that experience?
- ❖ What does baptism mean to you?

Action Items

- ❖ Find some water (preferably outside, but inside is fine too) and spend some time honoring your baptism.
- ❖ Do something extra to cultivate your spiritual life today: a bit of extra prayer time, finding a labyrinth to walk, some sitting meditation, singing–whatever fills your spirit with joy!
- ❖ Do something tangible to extend a sense of welcome to someone who might be feeling left out of a community you belong to. Whether this is someone in Sanctuary Collective, your church, or at work, do something to let them know they belong.

Day Forty
Nothing Can Separate You From God's Love

If you have time, read ROMANS 8:18-39 in your favorite Bible translation then come back to this page.

If you're short on time read this and pay attention to what jumps out at you as you read:

> *Who will bring a charge against God's elect people? It is God who acquits them. Who is going to convict them? It is Christ Jesus who died, even more, who was raised, and who also is at God's right side. It is Christ Jesus who also pleads our case for us.*
>
> *Who will separate us from Christ's love? Will we be separated by trouble, or distress, or harassment, or famine, or nakedness, or danger, or sword? As it is written,*
>
> *We are being put to death all day long for your sake.*
> *We are treated like sheep for slaughter.* [a]
>
> *But in all these things we win a sweeping victory through the one who loved us. I'm convinced that nothing can separate us from God's love in Christ Jesus our Lord: not death or life, not angels or rulers, not present things or future things, not powers or height or depth, or any other thing that is created.*
>
> **Romans 8:33-39**

SOMETIMES THERE ARE PASSAGES WE DON'T EVEN NEED TO QUEER in order to claim. They just exist and speak a word of comfort and healing to our hearts. These words from Romans are a reminder that we don't always have to come to the Bible with our defenses up, that throughout the pages we find words of inclusion and hope for us. All of us. No matter who we are, no matter where we live, no matter our orientation or gender identity or relationship status. We are good and loved, just as we are.

Some days (most days?) we need this reminder: Nothing can separate us from God. Not our parents or our partners. Not the rules of the church. Not what we've done in the past. Nothing. We don't even have to do anything to be a part of God's love. We don't even have to trust it because it's just there.

So lean in. Luxuriate in a feeling of safety and security.

You are loved. Nothing can take that away.

Journal Prompts

- ❖ What does it feel like (in your body) to hear that nothing can separate you from God?
- ❖ Journal about a time when you DID feel separate from God. What caused the feeling? How did you get past it?
- ❖ If you know nothing can separate you from God, what will your life look like as you really trust that knowing?

Action Items

- ❖ Make a list of things specific to your life you think could separate you from God. Then writing NOTHING over the top.
- ❖ Put the verse "Nothing can separate me from the love of God" in a place where you'll see it each day as a reminder.
- ❖ Reach out to someone who is struggling with their faith and remind them that nothing can separate them from the love of God.

What's Next On Your Journey?

We hope that this forty-day journey has been enriching and rewarding! You might be wondering what's next?

Here are a few ideas:

Sign up for Daily Affirmations. Get an email every weekday with a quote and some journaling prompts. These quotes are from the Bible, but also from activists, theologians, creatives, and so much more.
Sign up for free at queertheology.com/daily

Join Sanctuary Collective. A worldwide community of LGBTQ+ Christians and straight, cisgender supporters who are doing life together. You'll get access to online courses, digital magazines, and so much more. Plus, the opportunity to connect and walk with people from around the world who are diving deep into issues of faith.
Register at queertheology.com/community

Listen to the Queer Theology Podcast. Too often, the same 7 "clobber passages" are all that's discussed when it comes to LGBT lives and issues. We are more than what we are not. Each week at Queer Theology, we take a passage from the upcoming Sunday's lectionary and share a queer perspective on it. We think that looking at what Bible passages might say for LGBT people and what LGBT people might bring to passages are both important.
Listen & Subscribe at queertheology.com/listen

Explore even more resources at queertheology.com

Connect with us on social media. Look up "Queer Theology" or visit queertheology.com/social for direct links to all of our social media profiles.

We're so excited to continue journeying with you.

More About The Authors & QueerTheology.com

Brian G. Murphy

Brian G. Murphy is an activist, educator, and certified relationship coach.

For the past decade, he has worked on social justice and faith-based activism. He participated in the 2007 Soulforce Equality Ride, co-founded Legalize Trans, and most recently partnered with Fr. Shannon Kearns to create QueerTheology.com.

Through his work as a coach and content creator, Brian helps LGBTQ+ people claim their sexuality and gender, set healthy boundaries, develop meaningful spiritual practices, and step into an ever-more fulfilling life, all the while spreading the good news of the queer gospel to straight, cisgender Christians as well.

Brian has spoken about faith, sexuality, gender and justice at dozens of colleges and conferences across the USA.

Fr. Shannon TL Kearns

Father Shannon TL Kearns is a transgender man whose playwriting is obsessed with big questions told through small stories. He is a playwright, Artistic Director, sometimes actor, speaker, priest, and theologian. He is committed to work by and for marginalized communities, using writing to create a new future for all of us. Father Shannon TL Kearns is a seminary graduate (M.Div 2009 from Union Theological Seminary in the city of New York). He is a Priest in the Old Catholic Church. Shannon is the founder and Artistic Director of Uprising Theatre Company in Minneapolis, MN. He is the co-founder of QueerTheology.com. He was a Finnovation Fellow in 2019/2020, a Lambda Literary Fellow in 2019, and is a Playwrights' Center Jerome Fellow for 2020/2021.

The Queer Theology Team

When Brian G. Murphy and Fr. Shannon TL Kearns started QueerTheology.com in 2013, the prevailing conversation on LGBTQ+ issues and Christianity was narrowly focused on "apologetics"—that is, making the case that "it's ok" to be LGBTQ+ and Christian. Books like Torn by Justin Lee (2012) and God and the Gay Christian by Matthew Vines (2014) rehashed the same arguments that authors and theologians have been making for decades.

Something new was needed.

QueerTheology.com set out to make the work of queer theology academics accessible and useful to everyday Christians, both queer and not.

Brian G. Murphy and Fr. Shannon TL Kearns started something new with the conversation at the intersections of LGBTQ+ lives and Christianity — focusing on the inherent goodness and the unique gifts and blessings of queerness, rather than reacting against what we are not.

Together, they've started and broken open conversations around

- Purity culture
- Sex-positivity
- Queer bodies
- Transgender theology
- The interplay between Queer activism and Christian activism (from Palm Sunday to ACT UP)
- Christianity & Polyamory
- and more

Their message has reached over 1,000,000 people in over 200 countries and territories through their website, podcast, and videos.

More than that, it's inspired a new way to talk about gender, sexuality, and justice that has been replicated by others including hashtags, books, podcasts, and apps. They have forever changed the public discourse around queerness and Christianity.